PLAYS FOR THE POOR THEATRE

The Saliva Milkshake, Christie in Love, Gum and Goo, Heads, The Education of Skinny Spew

These five short plays are from Brenton's early involvement in such 'shoestring' groups as Portable Theatre. They are deliberately intended for the 'poor theatre' – as relevant today as when they were first written – since each play requires a small cast and minimal set, yet yields maximum theatricality.

Christie in Love, Gum and Goo, Heads and *The Education of Skinny Spew* were all first staged in 1969. *The Saliva Milkshake* was first staged in 1975.

'The theme of this taut, sharp, melancholic melodrama . . . is the way the fire in the belly of the sixties revolutionaries has turned into a fitful liberal flicker in the sedate seventies.'

(of *Saliva Milkshake*)   Michael Billington, *Guardian*

Howard Brenton was born in Portsmouth in 1942 and educated in Chichester and at St Catherine's College, Cambridge. In 1966 he joined the Brighton Combination as an actor and writer, and in 1969 he joined David Hare and Tony Bicat in Portable Theatre. His first full-length play was *Revenge* (1969) which was performed at the Royal Court Upstairs; this was followed by *Hitler Dances* (1972); *Magnificence* (1973); *Brassneck* (with David Hare, 1973); *The Churchill Play* (1974); *Weapons of Happiness* (winner of the Evening Standard Award, 1976); *Epsom Downs* (1977); *Sore Throats* (1979); *The Life of Galileo* (from Bertolt Brecht, 1980); *The Romans in Britain* (1980); *Thirteenth Night* (1981); *Danton's Death* (from Büchner, 1982); *Bloody Poetry* (1984); *Desert of Lies* (1984). His four-part thriller *Dead Head* was broadcast by BBC 2 in 1986.

The photograph on the front cover shows a detail from Een Cluyte van Plaeyenwater *by Pieter Bʳˡ....... ...* ced *by courtesy of the* Rijkmu... *photograph of Howard Brenton* ... *reproduced by courtesy of Snoo* ...

HOWARD BRENTON

Plays for the Poor Theatre

THE SALIVA MILKSHAKE
CHRISTIE IN LOVE
GUM AND GOO
HEADS
THE EDUCATION OF
SKINNY SPEW

A METHUEN PAPERBACK

A METHUEN PAPERBACK

This collection first published in 1980 by Eyre Methuen Ltd.,
11 New Fetter Lane, London EC4P 4EE
Reprinted 1983 by Methuen London Ltd.
The Saliva Milkshake first published by TQ Publications in 1977
Christie in Love, Heads, The Education of Skinny Spew first
published by Methuen & Co Ltd in 1970
Gum and Goo first published by Eyre Methuen Ltd in 1972

The Saliva Milkshake © 1977 by Howard Brenton
Christie in Love, Heads, The Education of Skinny Spew © 1970 by
Howard Brenton
Gum and Goo © 1972 by Howard Brenton
This collection © 1980 by Howard Brenton
Reprinted 1988
ISBN 0 413 47080 6

Printed in Great Britain by
Richard Clay Ltd, Bungay, Suffolk

Set in IBM 10pt Journal by 𝖠 Tek-Art Ltd, Croydon, Surrey

Contents

Author's Note

Theatre takes place all the time. We *do it* all the time. It is not an
art exclusive to massive stages graced by highly trained actors
beneath massed lights. As most of us will sing a few notes during
the day and song is not exclusive to a concert hall or opera house,
so theatre is part of our daily discourse with each other. When you
tell a joke, the day's events to a friend or loved one, when you
set out to tell a truth or a lie — you set up a theatre.

These five plays in varied ways try to turn 'bad theatrical
conditions' to advantage. They are not easy to do or constricted
in what they say — their 'poverty' is that of theatre companies
with no money, amateur acting, touring conditions that can vary
from a studio theatre to a school gymnasium, to a room with a
bare floor and no electric plug.

I have been and will go on trying to write big plays — 'Magic
Flutes' and 'Boris Godonovs'. But that said, if the wreckers who
run this country at the moment strangle the possibility of big,
publicly financed theatre, playwrights and performers will not be
silenced. The poor theatre waits to be used. Theatre is the one
performing art that can be practised at the highest level of skill
and intensity naked of technology, its only instrument being —
ourselves.

H.B.

The Saliva Milkshake

The Saliva Milkshake was first presented at the Soho Poly Lunchtime Theatre on 23 June 1975. The cast was as follows:

MARTIN	Terry McGinity
JOAN	Angela Chadfield
RAFFETY	Dudley Sutton
SIR ROBERT	Stuart Barren

Directed by Robert Walker
Designed by Sue Blaine

MARTIN. The night they killed the Home Secretary, I got back to my flat at eight o'clock. (*A pause.*) Joan was there.

MARTIN *turns.* JOAN *is there.*

JOAN. Hello, Martin. Long time. (*A pause.*) Oh I broke in. Credit card. (*She flicks her wrist.*) Sorry. You're angry.

MARTIN. No . . .

JOAN. You're angry.

MARTIN. It's . . . A surprise.

JOAN. Close the door.

MARTIN. What? Oh.

MARTIN *turns away then back to her.*

JOAN. Cold.

MARTIN. November.

JOAN. What?

MARTIN. It's November.

JOAN. I've been waiting an hour.

MARTIN. Sorry.

JOAN. Don't apologize. I am a burglar.

MARTIN. Yes.

JOAN (*carefully*). A friend told me you are to be a mighty man of science.

MARTIN (*shrugs*). What about you?

JOAN. One more sociologist on the Graduate dung hill. I'm training to be a teacher.

MARTIN. That's . . .

JOAN. You're right. Nothing. Makes you wonder why they snatched you from the cradle, stuffed all those ideas into your head. You just end up unemployable. Eh?

MARTIN (*awkward, a pause*). Well.

JOAN. Well.

MARTIN. Do you still see Hal?

JOAN. Who?

MARTIN. Haldine.

JOAN. Oh. No.

A pause.

MARTIN. I'll make some coffee.

JOAN. I made some, actually.

MARTIN. Oh.

JOAN. It's still hot. In the kitchen.

MARTIN. Good.

JOAN. Black.

MARTIN. What?

JOAN. I'll have mine black, please.

MARTIN. Good.

MARTIN *goes out. A long pause.* MARTIN *comes back holding a percolator, two coffee mugs and a bottle of milk.*

JOAN. I killed the man. (*A pause.*) The Home Secretary. (*A pause.*) Of England, Scotland, Wales and Northern Ireland. Outside his home. He was getting into his car. And I shot him. (*A pause.*) It was . . . No, I'll spare you that. No, I won't. It was disgusting. (*A pause.*) We drove to his home. His home's in Hampstead. Very . . . White windows. Behind a wall, with trees. And a brass lantern with an electric bulb. (*A little laugh.*) Didn't even know if he'd be there. It was getting dark. We parked the car. And, in a few seconds, there he was. Funny, about public men. When you see them. As if . . . They've got a rainbow round them. An edge, between the air and the space they fill. As if they're not quite . . . In space. Our space. 'Spose in a way they're not. Anyway, I got out of the car, walked across the road and shot him. The Special Branch man was at the door of the house. With a suit case. (*A pause.*) In the evening paper . . . Said the Home Secretary was leaving for the weekend, in the country. With his wife. I didn't see her. Perhaps she was behind the Special Branch man in the hall. In the . . . (*A pause.*) Dark hallway.

Where was I? (*Miserable.*) Where was I? (*A pause.*) Ran back over the road. Into our car. Dropped me off at a tube. Swiss Cottage. Bakerloo . . . Line. Got out at Charing Cross. Had a pie. At the stall there, the taxi drivers use. Martin? Walked to Victoria. 'Long the Embankment. Parliament Square. Victoria Street. Got the Victoria Line. To Highbury. And . . . (*She shrugs.*) You.

MARTIN. Joan, are you joking?

JOAN. No joke. (*From her bag she takes the gun.*) It isn't loaded. They took the unfired rounds off me. But left me to get rid of the gun.

MARTIN. Jesus Christ, Joan. Jesus.

JOAN. There's a man.

MARTIN (*dully*). There's a man.

JOAN. He's got a passport for me. In another name.

MARTIN. He's got a passport for you. In another name.

JOAN. He works in the market in Northcote Road.

MARTIN. Oh?

JOAN. Near where you used to live. Clapham Junction.

MARTIN. Oh.

JOAN. His name's Johnny. He does vegetables.

MARTIN. Vegetables.

JOAN. He keeps his barrow in Kingdom Street. That's a little alley, right by the side of the Viaduct.

MARTIN *closes his eyes, stretches his eyebrows with fatigue.*

JOAN. Go under the Viaduct. With the white tiles on the wall.

MARTIN. Go?

JOAN (*ignores that*). Then first left. It's just an alley. His shed is the third along. If there's anything fishy, just walk on. The alley comes out on a new estate. He'll be there at half past nine. (*Lightly.*) The passport's got a photograph of me with a wig on, see? (*From her bag, she takes a polystyrene wig block, shaped like a head. The wig is in brown paper.*) Have to comb it a bit. (*She strokes the wig.*) Didn't give me the passport before, before . . .

MARTIN. Before you murdered the man.

JOAN. Before I murdered the man.

They're looking straight at each other.

JOAN. It's a matter of discipline. If I'd have been taken, and had the passport, it would have been a waste.

MARTIN. This is England! England!

JOAN. And Ireland.

MARTIN. Yes. But . . .

JOAN. You'd not have said 'But' when we were students.

MARTIN. No?

JOAN. No.

MARTIN. No. (*He smiles.*) No.

JOAN *frowns, but then smiles.* MARTIN *stops smiling.*

JOAN. Are you still a revolutionary socialist? (MARTIN *about to shrug.*) Johnny will be there at half past nine. The police know me. I've no one else to go to. If they're watching Johnny's place, and I turn up . . . (*A gesture.*) But they don't know you. We're not linked. You see why I've come to you. We're . . . Unsullied.

MARTIN. Unsullied.

A pause. Then she puts the polystyrene head into her bag, standing.

JOAN. Sorry. Sorry. I'm dreadfully sorry. I'll go.

MARTIN. No! (*Then very unsure.*) No . . .

MARTIN *aside. As he speaks, she mouths a sentence, wordlessly. It's 'Are you for us or are you against us?'*

MARTIN. I couldn't tell her . . . Get out. I felt . . . guilty. She thought I was a revolutionary. I was not. I never had been.

JOAN *mouths silently. 'The world must change. Our minds like a fist.'*

MARTIN. She began to talk. Urgently. Of her 'Revolution.' I didn't understand. I was only aware of her. She was too close to me. Physically. Her body. Not sexual . . . Oppressive. Her personality. I tried . . . To see the world as she saw it. In her argument. In the words as she spoke them. But I couldn't. It was only her, going on and on. I wanted to scream. Get out. Oh, go, go. I can't breathe. You're sweating. You're too close. Get away from me. You're bullying me, you're smothering . . . You smell, you're sweating. . . You harp too much, you go on and oh . . .

JOAN *mouths silently* — '*The bourgeoisie doesn't sing*' — *wetly*. MARTIN *aside*.

MARTIN. She spat a little. A little saliva. I realised how wet the inside of her lip was. How close her teeth were and impervious to the juices of her mouth . . . That in her chin there must be a runnel . . . Below her lower lip . . . Gutter, lake, swamp, with the juices . . . Swishing . . . I became obsessed with this trivial, physical particularity . . . Her wet mouth . . . I couldn't follow what she was saying. I wanted to take a straw, milk straw, and suck out the wet. I fantasised on this. She was speaking of England and Ireland . . . Terror, abuse of working people . . . The long warp of religion and class warfare and . . . I could only think of her mouth. Little pumps, irrigation systems. A saliva milkshake. I'm not a political person.

JOAN. Will you go?

MARTIN. Why not? (*Aside*.) I couldn't say no. I was too ashamed. She trusted me. She'd told me she was . . . Murderer, assassin, criminal . . . Oh. Terrorist. Oh. And all I could think of, there and then, was . . . (*He wipes his mouth.*)

JOAN. Are you fatter?

MARTIN. Yes. I gave up smoking.

JOAN. You can taste things now.

MARTIN. Yes. It's . . . fun. (*A pause.*) I better be . . .

JOAN (*she interrupts*). Do you . . . (*She laughs. Nervously.*) Do you know I can't stop thinking of pop songs. I look at the world and I notice it's turning.

MARTIN. I'll be back in an hour, hour and a half.

JOAN. Yes. (*A pause.*) Walk me out in the morning dew.

MARTIN (*aside*). Plunged. Just plunged out that night. Into London. Highbury and Islington tube. Victoria line. Got off at Victoria. Surface train to Clapham Junction. Coming up the escalator at Victoria, to my left, bras in freedom positions.

Our society is mad, the man on the TV said. Thought of running amok . . . Girl in front of me, full bum . . . Thought of running amok, had a hard on . . . And at Capham Junction. Under the viaduct with the white tiles. Shed Agro. The alley. Dogshit. The people of a nearby tenement put out their dustbins there.

He falls over a dustbin. A cat screeches. Dogs set up a chain of barks. These animal sounds are made live by the other actors. MARTIN *lies and listens.*

MARTIN. Three along.

JOHNNY *sits in a dark corner amongst boxes of vegetables.* JOHNNY *looks straight at* MARTIN.

MARTIN. Johnny?

JOHNNY. Oh boy.

MARTIN. Are you Johnny?

JOHNNY. Oh boy.

MARTIN. Joan . . . Joan. She sent me. About . . . She sent me. About, for . . . The passport.

JOHNNY. Christ, but it's snowing hard.

MARTIN. What? (MARTIN *looks hard at* JOHNNY.) Stoned. (MARTIN *turns the shed over throwing things about.*) I was angry. Felt . . . Righteous. Crossed London, scared . . . For what? To stoop into a dirty shed to find some Irishman zonked out of his mind. The terrifying thought . . . Maybe they don't know what they're doing. (MARTIN *threatens* JOHNNY *with a cabbage.*) Passport for Joan, Joan.

JOHNNY (*calmly*). My name's not Joan.

MARTIN. I've come for her passport.

JOHNNY. The bloody Tsar of all the Russians, eating human flesh in the snow.

MARTIN *hunts through* JOHNNY's *pockets.* JOHNNY *lets him.* MARTIN *finds nothing, sits back on his haunches and pinches the bridge of his nose, tired.*

JOHNNY. Millions of 'em. Over the snowfields. Trying to crawl away. (*He looks at* MARTIN.) Russia? Bloody Russia? (*He cries. Closes his eyes. Turns his head away.*)

MARTIN (*aside*). Walked away. North. A lot of yellow light.
Came, in the end, to the Thames. Battersea Fun Fair. Depot
for buses. And on the other side of the road, a place where
they made milk bottles. Not a thought in my head. Didn't
know how long I'd walked. Never wear a watch. May interfere
with instruments, in the lab. Half an hour? Hour? Traffic over
Chelsea Bridge. Or was it Battersea Bridge? Power Station . . .
(*Passionately*.) And I hated Joan. Mid-evening. London traffic
going North and South . . . (*Calmly*.) And decided to betray
her. Naturally I was tired, I ached . . . And I betrayed her.
Effortlessly. Without constriction of conscience. Simple as
breathing. Streets are streets. England's England. (*Passionately*.)
The bitch, the bitch . . . With her lurid, selfish . . . Slimy,
evil . . . View of the world . . . In my room. My things. Coming
all over me. I didn't ask her to. I didn't want her to. (*Calmly
again*.) Got a taxi, and went to see the Professor who had
taught me.

MARTIN *turns*. SIR ROBERT *comes on. Off, voices of a
dinner party. Three* GUESTS — *the third is a woman.*

GUEST 1. Never really to grips.

GUEST 2. No.

GUEST 1. Would you call him soft?

SIR ROBERT. Martin. This is bloody inconvenient.

GUEST 3. Mellowed and melted.

SIR ROBERT. Got a dinner party.

MARTIN (*aside*). Told him.

SIR ROBERT *stares at* MARTIN.

GUEST 1. But lung tissue's like that.

GUEST 2. Chemical change . . .

GUEST 1. Difficult to grip . . .

GUEST 3. Superbly alive, though.

SIR ROBERT. The silly little cow's not joking?

MARTIN. No.

SIR ROBERT. And she's sitting in your room. Now.

MARTIN. Yes.

GUEST 2. Osmotic?

GUEST 1. Not really. Not really at all.

GUEST 3. His bottom was very low slung. (*Laughter.*)

SIR ROBERT. We'll go. Now.

MARTIN. I'm very sorry to disturb you.

SIR ROBERT (*incredulous*). A member of the government's been murdered, Martin.

MARTIN (*deliberately aside*). Telephone call . . . Sir Robert's car . . . Power driven windows . . . He didn't speak much. I'm an orphan, he was a man to whom I'd been grateful . . . I knew he'd been in Intelligence during the war. . . We went to a house, a building, near Green Park. Had a revolving door, like a hotel. (*They mime going through a door.*) But inside was a double door. Locked. With a grill. And guarded by a man in a suit.

SIR ROBERT. Would you please tell Mr. Raffety Sir Robert is here.

MARTIN (*aside*). And in a little while the man in the suit let us in, and led us up to the first floor. I could just, if I tried, hear the London traffic.

MARTIN *turns.* RAFFETY *is there.* SIR ROBERT *sits in a chair to one side.* RAFFETY *blows his cheeks up then lets the air come out.*

RAFFETY. When did you see her last? Before she plopped herself on your floor . . . (*Looks at his watch.*) Two and three quarter hours ago?

MARTIN. I told you. Two years ago, at least . . .

RAFFETY. And there she is. Plop.

MARTIN. Yes.

RAFFETY. Saying 'With my little gun I killed the Home Secretary.'

MARTIN. Yes.

RAFFETY. Are you a liberal, Martin?

MARTIN. What?

RAFFETY ?

MARTIN. I suppose so. Perhaps. Yes. Why not?

RAFFETY. She thinks you are a revolutionary socialist. Of some hue. But revolutionary . . . With a like mind.

MARTIN. She's wrong.

RAFFETY. Is she?

MARTIN. Yes!

RAFFETY. Tragically wrong for her, then.

MARTIN. I came here . . . I don't believe in murder.

RAFFETY. Killing people is wrong?

MARTIN. Isn't it?

RAFFETY. No. Not at all.

MARTIN. I . . .

RAFFETY. No, we're grateful. You did a good service to your country. (*A pause*.) Martin. It can't be easy to betray a friend. Ever sleep with her?

MARTIN. No!

RAFFETY. Good.

A pause.

MARTIN. Paranoia.

RAFFETY. What, old son?

MARTIN. I feel paranoid.

RAFFETY. Why?

MARTIN. You think I'm guilty in some way.

RAFFETY. Guilty?

MARTIN. Tainted.

RAFFETY. Do I?

MARTIN. I can feel it. In your voice . . . Feel it, in the drift . . . In your drift.

RAFFETY. Mmm.

MARTIN. What do you mean by that?

RAFFETY. By mmm?

MARTIN. Sir Robert . . .

MARTIN *looks at* SIR ROBERT, *who looks down.* MARTIN *looks away then back at him, and catches* SIR ROBERT *looking at* RAFFETY. RAFFETY *laughs.*

RAFFETY. Forgive us, Martin. Sir Robert and I are old friends. So. What are we to do with your silly little murderess?

MARTIN. Take her.

RAFFETY. Take her?

MARTIN. Take her away.

RAFFETY. 'Out of your life?' (MARTIN *flinches.*) Sir Robert tells me you are brilliant. Or your work is.

MARTIN (*shrugs*). Yes.

RAFFETY. And that you are to be a professor. (MARTIN *looks sharply at* SIR ROBERT). Oh don't play naive. You know you're being thought of.

MARTIN. Yes.

RAFFETY. You're young for it.

MARTIN. Yes . . .

RAFFETY. And this affair . . .

A pause.

MARTIN. What? You *what*?

RAFFETY. Do you know the Devenish Chair has finance from the Ministry of Defense?

MARTIN. No.

RAFFETY. You do now.

MARTIN. It does not . . .

RAFFETY. Don't be silly. It's for warwork.

MARTIN. You're being silly.

RAFFETY. I speak the truth, don't I, Sir Robert?

MARTIN *looks at* SIR ROBERT, *who looks down.*

MARTIN. The Devenish Chair is independently financed . . . And you're saying the professor is obliged to . . . What? Make germs for the RAF?

RAFFETY. Yup. (*A pause.* MARTIN *non-plussed.*) Of course we only make this known to the successful candidate, after he has taken the chair.

MARTIN. You may end up with a raving Maoist.

RAFFETY. We make sure we don't. By the way, *you* will be asked to sign the Official Secrets Act on the way out of here.

MARTIN. I . . . Told you . . . About Joan . . . For my reasons. Moral reasons. I didn't think of my career.

RAFFETY. You may as well have.

MARTIN. You don't realise. I'm . . .

RAFFETY. What? Sincere? A nice person? (RAFFETY *smiles.*) How's the paranoia?

MARTIN. High.

RAFFETY. The hay fever of the liberal conscience. (SIR ROBERT *laughs.*) I thank you. (*He holds up a key.*) Key. To a luggage locker on Euston Station. Give the key to Joan and tell her the passport is in locker number 32.

MARTIN. Why?

RAFFETY ?

MARTIN. I mean why should Johnny leave the passport in a locker in Euston Station?

RAFFETY. I'm sure you'll work something out.

MARTIN. Thank you.

RAFFETY (*ignores that, earnestly*). Try and delay her. Take off her knickers or something. So she turns up late. That way there'll be less people in the Station. It's now . . . (*Looks at his watch.*) Pushing eleven-fifteen. You'd better get back to her. We appreciate your work. Thank you. (*And suddenly he's cross.*) Don't feel abused.

MARTIN (*aside*). Abused.

MARTIN *turns.* JOAN *comes on. Now she wears the wig.*

JOAN. You were a long time.

MARTIN. He didn't turn up for a while. Joan, he didn't have the passport.

A pause.

JOAN. Why not?

MARTIN. I don't know. (*A pause. Then* MARTIN *hands her the key.*) He sent this.

She looks at the key on the palm of her hand.

JOAN. A key.

MARTIN. For a luggage locker in Euston Station. Number 32. He left the passport there.

JOAN. Why did he do that?

MARTIN. I don't know!

JOAN. Was he stoned?

MARTIN. Yes. (*Quickly.*) I mean . . . Yes.

JOAN. Bloody idiot. (*Pause.*) Well. Thanks.

MARTIN. Yes. Joan, perhaps we should look beauty in the face.

A pause.

JOAN. You what?

MARTIN. Maybe we shouldn't be ashamed to look beauty in the face.

JOAN. What the hell does that mean?

MARTIN. I think we've got lost.

JOAN. Speak for yourself.

MARTIN. In violence . . .

A pause.

JOAN. Don't understand you.

MARTIN. We've got lost in violence. . . For Godsake, Joan, you killed a man.

JOAN (*gently*). And I should look beauty in the face?

MARTIN. It's all a fantasy, Joan. You . . . We . . . Meant well at first. But we got to a ghetto life . . . Ghetto life of ideas. The paranoia. The unreality . . . Mindburn, world change. Back in the 60's we were clever, hopeful and good. We had the politics of free. And the world was there for burning. All time factors in the now. Acid-zap, mind-moil, positive forces coming to now. The holy cancer, weren't we, eating the mother culture. But we got corrupted. Don't know by

what . . . Love of a lurid view of the world? But we did, we
got . . . Vicious. Lovers of plague. Dear God, if plague broke
out in England, now. I think many of my generation would
be glad.

JOAN. Martin, what are you talking about?

MARTIN. I . . . I . . . (*Shakes his head.*) Excess of nightmare.
Good, middle-class children of the nineteen-sixties. Drowning
in the blood . . . Of a man you killed today, Joan.

JOAN. It's a war, Martin.

MARTIN. I was in Paris, last autumn. I met a man . . . Our age.
He'd been a student in Paris during May, 1968. A splinter of
glass had injured his eye during the riots. He said to me . . .
We're a dead generation now.

JOAN. It's . . . A . . . Class . . . War.

MARTIN. Don't you believe in anything human? Or tender?

JOAN. You're childish.

MARTIN. That's not good enough!

JOAN. I'm tired.

MARTIN (*near tears*). Don't you believe in anything?

JOAN (*in a sing-song*). A land . . . Without want. Without
ignorance. A land of science. Abundance. Democracy and
peace. And . . . A bloody, brutal ugly business getting it, Martin.
(*A pause.*) I better go. (*She holds the keys up.*) This real?
(*Nothing from* MARTIN.) So long. (*She's going but turns.*)
Sorry to come in on you. Out of nowhere. Thanks for the
help.

She goes leaving the wig block on the floor. MARTIN *looks
at it and speaks aside.*

MARTIN. Didn't sleep. Turned on the radio. Nightride, twelve
to two. Fumbling through the Muzak . . . News, news . . .
The Scene at Euston Station. Broken glass, head on the
concrete, pool of blood. After two o'clock, turned to the
commercial stations. Nothing of her. Phone-ins all night. Had
she taken fright? When I babbled to her . . . Beauty in the
face? What had I meant by that? I know, I meant . . . I'm
sick, sick with fear. The world is blowing up . . . She knew.
She'd not go anywhere near the thirty-second luggage locker

in Euston Station. Not that tight little bitch. Not that
murdering tart. No, not a chance . . . (*He looks at the wig
block.*) Five a.m. Couldn't stand it. Rushed out. Imagining
the locker. Bright. Steel. Ran through the street. To Euston.
Bright, all glass, glass in the eye . . . Chickened out. Couldn't
go in. Stood on the forecourt, glass cliff of the railway station
in front of me. Dare not. Walked home. Bought ten Players
in a machine. Got home at half past six. Lit a cigarette. It
was the ninety-seventh day since I had given up. Turned on
the radio. News on the half hour. They'd rushed Joan at
Euston Station. The gun had been loaded. She wounded
herself, through the mouth, into her brain.

A pause as MARTIN *lights a cigarette. During the remainder
of this speech he picks up the polystyrene wig block and
burns a face into it with his cigarette. The mouth of the face
is straight, neither sad or laughing.*

She didn't die at first, though she was never conscious. It was
'News on the Hour', Radio 1, I heard . . . Four o'clock that
following afternoon, she had died. For a little while, perhaps
two days . . . It was as if her murder and suicide . . . stained the
quality of life. Like the night they let the car bombs off. And
going south of the river, Camberwell Bus Depot, that night,
we the passengers saw a bus on fire. And felt the underswell,
the paranoia . . . It was that way after Joan. (*Stubs the
cigarette out.*) Three days, then, in my flat. Holed up . . .
Couldn't go out. In the end, forced to, for fags . . . Pleaded
migraine to the College . . . Longed for migraine, though I
have never been a sufferer . . . The split, the old brain slice,
wire in the cheese, oh ho ho. Red. Hot. (*A pause.*) Went back
to work. Three weeks. Dulled, dulled. (*Change.*) Then one
lunchtime a student of mine said to me . . . You know her,
don't you? What do you mean I said? *Out of my mind* . . . A
lot of us admire your stand, he said. I wanted to hit him in
the face. And the next day Raffety sent for me.

MARTIN *turns.* RAFFETY *comes on.*

RAFFETY. Joan was a Maoist. There was a group. They had
situationist tendencies. (MARTIN *raises an eyebrow.*)
Forgive me. Special Branch and the extremist groups share a
vocabulary . . . We're both in a world of our own, really.
Situationist tendencies . . . Notions of anarchic display.

MARTIN. Ah.

RAFFETY. Wall posters. Demonstrations. Festivals, fireworks.
Assassinations. Dancing in the streets. Sabotage. The politics
of free. Celebrations. That kind of thing. (*Looks at* MARTIN,
quizzically, then continues.) There were five in Joan's group.
One was Irish. You met him. Not a barrow boy, by the way,
but a mathematician from Imperial College. Joan's group
admired the Official Wing of the Irish Republican Army.
Fancied their politics, particularly the mass democracy line,
Maoist style. Joan's group approached the Officials. Who told
them where to put their . . . Armageddons? But . . . The idea
of a link between English, ex-student extremists and the old
Irish firms . . . Tickles us. (*A pause.*) Fill you in. So you don't
feel too . . . Lonely? (*A pause.*) You've lost weight.

MARTIN. I'm smoking. Gone back to it.

RAFFETY. Cuts oxygen, y'know.

MARTIN. All that . . .

RAFFETY ?

MARTIN. Double dutch to me. Can I go now?

RAFFETY. Martin, do you think people are getting at you?
Well, they're not.

MARTIN. I can go?

RAFFETY. Why did you go to Kingdom Street? Put that another
way. If Johnny had not been incapacitated and had had the
passport . . . Would you have taken it? All the way back to
Joan? (*A pause.*) See, like many a Liberal Conscience you
dallied that night, you . . . Swung on a hair's breadth. Fifteen
years in gaol were with you that night. There's a tickle in that
for us, too. Fortunately you sent the girl to her . . . End.
(*Compassionately.*) The pain won't go away, Martin. (*He sits
back. Calmly.*) Anyone spoken to you in the last few days . . .
about Joan? (*Nothing from* MARTIN.) Let us know when they
do. . . For they will. (*A pause.*) Serve your Queen and country.
Or, if you want to put it that way, serve English Capitalism
and our South African investments. (*He grins.*) I do. With all
my heart.

MARTIN. This is England, England. Not a police state.

RAFFETY. That . . . Depends who you are. Don't leave London.

I mean, you're not going away, are you?

MARTIN (*shrugs*). Where to?

RAFFETY. Where to.

MARTIN (*aside*). Where to. (*A pause. Then quickly, to the end.*) They came to see me, three days later. They thought I was a hero. They looked up to me. They asked my advice. They trusted me. I couldn't bear it. Their unreality.

MARTIN *is confronted by two men.*

I confessed. Told them I betrayed . . . I leant against the wall. Calm, free. For a moment at rights with the world. (*A pause.*) Then they punished me.

The two men step forward to MARTIN *and bring him forward.*

They punctured my ear drums. Now I'm deaf. (*A pause.*) What? (*A pause.*) What did you say? (*A pause.*) What? (*A pause.*) What?

Christie in Love

Author's Production Note

CHRISTIE's first appearance is in the Dracula tradition. Happy horror, creeps and treats. He rises from the grave luridly, in a frightening mask. It looks as if a juicy evening's underway, all laughs, nice shivers, easy oohs and aahs.

But that's smashed up. The lights are slammed on, and the mask is seen as only a tatty bit of papier mâché. Off it comes, and what's left is a feeble, ordinary man blinking through his pebble glasses.

The Publishers asked for a production note, and I'm setting down the devices I tried to use in the show. That's the basic one. A kind of dislocation, tearing one style up for another, so the proceedings lurch and all interpretations are blocked, and the spectator hunting for an easy meaning wearies, and is left only with CHRISTIE and his act of love.

The play is a black sketch if played fast, and I suppose it would be quite funny if done at that pace. But I categorically forbid anyone to do so. I want it to last nearly an hour. It is written to be played very slowly.

Any director who's nervous about this slowness, please look at the first scene. David Hare, in the Portable Theatre production, got it right and it was taking at least twenty minutes to play. Its an old trick after all, to play the first scene of a slow play very slowly. Once the first scene is established, the actors make judgements about the pauses and little rushes needed for the interrogation scenes.

The 'Garden' is a pen, ten feet by six feet. Its sides are two and a half feet high, and made of chicken wire. It's brim full of torn and screwed up pages of a popular newspaper. The spectators sit all around, and very close — there's barely enough room for the actors to walk round the sides. The pen is a filthy sight. The chicken wire is rusty, the wood is stained, the paper is full of dust. It's used as CHRISTIE's garden, his front room, a room in a police station, an executioner's shed, a lime pit. But it's not a 'Setting' in a conventional sense. I don't want it to be *like* a garden, or a room. It's a theatrical machine, a thing you'd only see in a show. It's a trap, a flypaper for the attention of the spectators to stick on.

The doll is a little larger than life size. She must not be in any way a pornographic object. She is dressed in a faded blue skirt and dirty white blouse of the early fifties, her skin is grey, her hair frizzy and short the way they wore it then. Her underwear is massive, unfrilly, not sexy. The CONSTABLE has to undress her — that scene's tricky and he must be able to strip her quickly. Valcro can be used instead of buttons and eyes.

The CONSTABLE and the INSPECTOR are not 'characters', apart from the facts of age and rank. (The INSPECTOR is in his mid-thirties, the CONSTABLE in his late twenties.) They are stage coppers. But they have 'sudden lights', unpredictable speeches beyond the confines of pastiche. As if a cardboard black and white cut-out suddenly reaches out a fully fleshed, real hand. It's a bathos technique (the end of HEADS works by it.) It is very cruel.

The artifice of the garden and the 'stage' nature of the police-men's parts are intended to throw the CHRISTIE part into relief. With CHRISTIE I tried to write a fully fledged naturalistic part.

I am greatly indebted to William Hoyland's playing of CHRISTIE. That the part is in a style radically different from that of the policemen is a fundamental dislocation in the play. Bill got it right. Over fifty performances with the Portable Theatre, in all kinds of conditions, he developed the part until it had an illusory effect. An obscene insolence — in the middle of all that artificial invention, all that tat, the garden, the doll, the role-playing coppers, sat Bill's CHRISTIE, 'believable', 'real'.

H.B.

Christie in Love was first performed by The Portable Theatre at Oval House, London, on 23 November 1969, with the following cast:

CHRISTIE   William Hoyland
CONSTABLE   Matthew Walters
INSPECTOR   Andrew Carr

Directed by David Hare
Stage Management by Snoo Wilson
Set built by Tony Bicat

It was later performed at the Royal Court Theatre Upstairs, London, on 12 March 1970 with the following cast:

CHRISTIE   William Hoyland
CONSTABLE   Brian Croucher
INSPECTOR   Stanley Lebor

Directed by David Hare
Stage Manager Betty Ritchie
Assistant Stage Managers Nick Hart, David Gotthard
Lighting by Gareth Jones

While the audience comes in, the CONSTABLE *actor digs in the garden, the* INSPECTOR *actor stands at the back, the* CHRISTIE *actor lies concealed beneath the newspaper. A tape broadcasts the facts again and again.*

TAPE. John Reginald Halliday Christie was born in Halifax, April of 1898.

He hated his mother, his father and his sisters.

His childhood was normal.

December of 1938, Christie moved with his wife to London.

His marriage was normal.

In March of 1953, Police arrested Christie for murder.

In Christie's London house, the Police found the following corpses.

Buried in the garden, a Miss Eady.

Buried in the garden, a Miss Fuerst.

Hanging in the concealed kitchen alcove, a Miss MacLennan.

Hanging in the concealed kitchen alcove, a Miss Maloney.

Hanging in the concealed kitchen alcove, a Miss Nelson.

Laid beneath the boards of the living-room floor, Mrs Ethel Christie.

Questioned, an old school mate said of Christie 'He kept himself to himself.'

Christie wrote 'As I gazed down at the still form of my first victim, I experienced a strange, peaceful thrill.'

Christie was hanged July of 1953.

When all the audience is in, the tape fades.

Scene One

The CONSTABLE *digs in the garden. Paper falls from the spade. He continues, very slowly, until everyone present is looking at the paper, as it falls from the spade. The* CONSTABLE *stops. He stares at the paper. He looks up, and around at the audience. He recites the first limerick. His recitation is uncomic, deadly.*

CONSTABLE. In the Garden of Eden lay Adam.

A pause.

In the Garden of Eden lay Adam
Complacently stroking his madam.
Very loud was his mirth,
For on all of the Earth,
There were only two balls, and he had 'em.

A pause. The CONSTABLE *reflects.*

There were only two balls, and he had 'em.

The CONSTABLE *nods to himself. He digs again. Paper falls from the spade. He stops digging, and looks up.*

There was a young girl named Heather.

A pause.

There was a young girl named Heather
Whose cunt was made out of leather.
She made an odd noise,
For attracting the boys,
By flapping the edges together.

A pause. The CONSTABLE *reflects.*

By flapping the edges together.

The CONSTABLE *nods to himself. He digs again. Paper falls from the spade. He stops digging, and looks up.*

A bawdy young rake from Tashkent.

A pause.

A bawdy young rake from Tashkent
Had a cock that was horribly bent.
To get over the trouble,
He pushed it in double,
And instead of his coming he went.

At once the INSPECTOR *shouts from the back. The* CONSTABLE *jerks to attention.*

INSPECTOR. Constable!

CONSTABLE. Sir!

INSPECTOR. What you doing!

CONSTABLE. Digging Sir!

INSPECTOR. Digging for what Constable!

CONSTABLE. Bones Sir!

INSPECTOR. Right! Bones!

CONSTABLE. Digging for bones Sir!

INSPECTOR. Right again! You keep bones on your mind!

CONSTABLE. I've got bones on my mind Sir!

INSPECTOR. Good man! You keep them there and you won't go far wrong!

A pause.

INSPECTOR. Get on with it then!

CONSTABLE. Sir!

The CONSTABLE *digs vigorously. After a while, he wearies, slows down and stops. He looks up.*

CONSTABLE. There was an odd fellow named West.

A pause.

There was an odd fellow named West
Whose cock came up to his chest.
He said 'I declare',
'I've got no pubic hair',
So he covered his balls with his vest.

INSPECTOR. Constable!

CONSTABLE. Sir!

INSPECTOR. Kind of bones!

A pause.

CONSTABLE. Sir?

INSPECTOR. What kind of bones you looking for? Bones of what animal? Of what genus or species?

CONSTABLE. Women's bones, in't it Sir? The bones of . . .

The CONSTABLE *searches for the word.*

Ladies?

INSPECTOR. Right. How very right you are. The bones of English Ladies. That's what he's been burying down there, somewhere. Burying English Ladies in his garden! We're going to do him for that!

CONSTABLE. We're going to do him for that Sir!

INSPECTOR. I've heard of some nasty things in my life. But burying English Ladies in your own backyard just about takes the candle. Dig 'em up!

CONSTABLE. Right!

The CONSTABLE *starts digging again, vigorously.*

Right!

INSPECTOR. First sign of a bone, give me the word.

CONSTABLE. Right!

INSPECTOR. The mothers of England depend on you.

The CONSTABLE *digs on. After a while, he wearies, slows down and stops. He looks up.*

CONSTABLE. There was a young man from Coombe.

A pause.

There was a young man from Coombe
Who was born six months too soon.
He hadn't the luck,
To be got from a fuck,
But a toss off shoved in with a spoon.

A pause. The CONSTABLE *reflects.*

A toss off. Shoved.

The CONSTABLE *shakes his head, appalled. He wipes his brow. The* INSPECTOR *comes from the back. Looks the garden over. Looks right and left to see if they are private. Takes out a flask, and offers the* CONSTABLE *a drink. The* CONSTABLE *hesitates, wary of rank, but accepts and sits on the side of the garden. The* INSPECTOR *actor tells the following joke in this way — he works out the pace of a bad joke teller, the abominable and humourless timing, and then exaggerates the pauses. He stretches it to breaking point.*

INSPECTOR. Know the one about the faith healer?

CONSTABLE. Actually, no Sir.

The INSPECTOR *looks around.*

INSPECTOR. Keep this to yourself.

CONSTABLE. Eh, yes Sir.

INSPECTOR. There was this faith healer you see.

A pause.

CONSTABLE. Sir?

INSPECTOR. Wait for it.

CONSTABLE. Yes Sir.

A pause.

INSPECTOR. There was this faith healer. The most famous in the land. Anything he touched, he . . .

A pause.

CONSTABLE. I see Sir.

INSPECTOR. Cured. He had what you'd call a wonderful touch.

A pause.

CONSTABLE. Cured, Sir.

INSPECTOR. Anyway, this faith healer, he got married. And the first time in bed with his wife he ran his hands all over her, and sealed her up.

A long pause.

INSPECTOR. Just a little joke between ourselves.

CONSTABLE. Yes Sir. Very funny Sir.

INSPECTOR. Get on with it.

The INSPECTOR *turns away.*

CONSTABLE. Bleeding hell.

The CONSTABLE *puts the spade in once. He stops dead still, staring down. Simultaneously the* INSPECTOR, *who was walking away, stops dead still. A pause. The* CONSTABLE *speaks quietly.*

Oh my God.

The INSPECTOR *turns. A pause. This passage very loudly.*

CONSTABLE. Bone Sir!

INSPECTOR. Bone!

CONSTABLE. Bone here Sir!

INSPECTOR. Bone there!

CONSTABLE. Got a bone here Sir!

INSPECTOR. What dug up a bone!

CONSTABLE. Bone here!

A pause. The CONSTABLE *speaks quietly.*

More than a bone.

The INSPECTOR *goes to see, climbs into the garden. This passage spoken ordinarily.*

What were she? Tart?

INSPECTOR. Who knows?

CONSTABLE. What he do to her?

The INSPECTOR *shrugs.*

INSPECTOR. What he wanted. No more, no less.

The CONSTABLE *gestures at the grave.*

CONSTABLE. It's beyond me. All that.

INSPECTOR. Takes all kinds. The General Public is a dirty animal.

CONSTABLE. It's beyond me.

INSPECTOR. Don't brood on it Lad. There're many ways of pleasure, most of 'em filth.

CONSTABLE. Still beyond me.

A pause.

Look at that fucking great slug.

At once the INSPECTOR *and the* CONSTABLE *stand back to back. They turn round on the audience in unison with each line, shouting out the limerick. They end facing each other, shaking with rage.*

INSPECTOR AND CONSTABLE. THERE WAS A YOUNG MAN FROM BENGAL
WHO WENT TO A FANCY DRESS BALL.
JUST FOR A STUNT,
HE WENT AS A CUNT,
AND WAS HAD BY A DOG IN THE HALL.

A pause.

INSPECTOR. Right. Let's pack up and get out of here.

The INSPECTOR *and the* CONSTABLE *climb out of the garden, and go to the back. They collect a stretcher and a tarpaulin sheet. They come back, open the stretcher beside the grave. They lay the tarpaulin over the corpse. From here, the lights begin a long fade to the end of the scene.*

CONSTABLE. Sir, what you reckon he did?

INSPECTOR. Did?

CONSTABLE. He whip 'em? Make 'em . . . Adopt poses? Stick feathers on 'em?

INSPECTOR. Lad, I'll give you a word of warning. I been on these pervy cases before. And the word of warning is, don't brood. You brood, and it'll get you down.

CONSTABLE. It could get you down.

INSPECTOR. It could.

CONSTABLE. It is already.

The CONSTABLE *feels his stomach.*

INSPECTOR. Now copper. Have a bash at controlling yourself.

CONSTABLE. I'll have a bash Sir.

INSPECTOR. Get her up.

They stand, the CONSTABLE *at the front of the stretcher, the* INSPECTOR *at the back.*

Come on my little darling.

They step out of the garden. They carry the corpse out to the back during this passage, with a funeral step. The light is nearly gone.

INSPECTOR. Pleasures of the General Public. You see them all, all the fads. How some like it hot, and some like it cold. How some like it live and some like it dead. And sometimes, why, your own fancy is tickled.

They stop.

INSPECTOR. We are human.

CONSTABLE. We are human.

They go on.

INSPECTOR. So don't brood. Just clear up the mess.

CONSTABLE. I'll do that Sir.

In near darkness.

INSPECTOR. Just clear up the mess.

It's a blackout.

Scene Two

The lights are snapped up. Very bright. The INSPECTOR *and the* CONSTABLE *are businesslike.*

INSPECTOR. Ladies and Gents, John Reginald Christie did six women in.

CONSTABLE. The manner in which they were done was not nice.

INSPECTOR. So if anyone feels sick, go ahead. Throw up. We won't mind.

CONSTABLE. If you want to spew, spew.

INSPECTOR. Right. Let's have a look at him shall we.

The INSPECTOR *nods to the stage management. Blackout.*

Scene Three

In the blackout.

INSPECTOR. Out you come Reg.

CONSTABLE. Come on out Reggie.

INSPECTOR. John Reginald Christie!

CONSTABLE. Mr Christie Sir, out you come like a good Sir.

INSPECTOR. Come on Reggie. Let's have a look at you.

The INSPECTOR *and the* CONSTABLE *switch hand lamps on. They let the beams flick over the garden. The tape begins. The* CHRISTIE *actor raises his hand out of the paper. A beam catches it, then whisks away. The lamps go out. Then come on and off, at the discretion of the actors. The* CHRISTIE *actor rises from the paper.*

He wears a grotesque mask, a papier mâché head that distorts his features. He undoes his fly, and takes out a length of rubber tubing. He lets down his trousers. He blows into the tube, the effect should be that CHRISTIE's *activities are obscured, the beams of the hand lamps do not allow the audience a good look. The taped speech is spoken by the* CHRISTIE *actor.*

TAPE. Love. Love. Reggie knows his mind 'bout love. And Reggie's never been a one for it. S'all bunk. S'all got up by women. Not that I can't handle them. Women. The bloody female. I'm a dab hand with the ways of love and women, when I want. Much of the time I don't want, that's all. Bah. They give me the pip. Women. With little women's things. Brushes. Tweezers. Sanitary towels. Hairclips. Nasty little instruments to cut you. Coming at you with teeth to give you bites. They're violent, women are. The bitches! Coming up to you, getting violent. Start to paw you about. Get you doing things to them. And they doing things to you. My mother cut my hair. Very, very short. Came at me with scissors, the bitch. Gouging. Cutting off my length. I am a private man and I know my rights. I am, also, a dark horse. Women women women . . . The streets are full of them. In their nasty skirts. You can hear their skirts, rustle rustle. And their shoes like little metal rats, clip clip upon the pavement. All over. And their beady eyes sweeping the area like birds of prey. And their nails folded ready. They're on the look out! Women out at night for men. Scissors in their handbags to cut you off. Slice you where you're private. Each tit a nail to make you bleed. Each mouth a mousetrap. Cheese nearly in your chops when click! Back's broke. And each cunt a bacon slicer whittling manhood away. A woman's body that's a machine for death.

Panting breaths, the CHRISTIE *actor at climax in the garden. Then he throws himself full length. The handlamps go out. Silence. Then the tape continues.*

I am not worried. I know what I like. It is no trouble. It is lovely. It is . . .

A pause.

Cooling.

Scene Four

The lights snap on. CHRISTIE *with his trousers down. He takes off the head, and blinks. Then buries it. The* INSPECTOR *is standing by the garden, looking on.*

INSPECTOR. Presentable yet, Reg?

A pause.

I don't want to bother you if you're not . . .

A pause.

Presentable.

CHRISTIE *blinks at him. Hurriedly pulls up his trousers, does up the fly.*

CHRISTIE. I'm all right. Thank you very much.

INSPECTOR. Oh! You're all right.

A pause.

CHRISTIE. I am.

A pause.

INSPECTOR. Let's get on with it then.

The INSPECTOR *quickly goes to the back, and comes forward with a battered card table and a battered wooden chair. He sets them in the garden.*

INSPECTOR. Take a chair.

CHRISTIE. Oh. Right.

CHRISTIE *sits on the chair.*

INSPECTOR. Right!

A pause.

Good. There we are then. That's it.

A pause.

Then. Good.

A pause.

Then.

A pause.

Ten Rillington Place.

A pause.

Your property?

CHRISTIE. My property.

INSPECTOR. Oh, it's *your* property.

CHRISTIE. That's my home.

INSPECTOR. But I thought you rented.

A pause.

I thought you were a rent-paying tenant. OF the property.

CHRISTIE. The house is my home.

INSPECTOR. Your rented home.

CHRISTIE. I said. The house is my home.

INSPECTOR. But the freehold. That's not yours. Reggie I can't see, I mean I cannot understand, why you are reluctant to admit that you pay rent. I'm speaking frankly now.

CHRISTIE. Oh ay.

INSPECTOR. Are you saying, you fancy yourself as the landlord?

A pause.

You fancy you are a property developer?

The INSPECTOR *smiles, chuckles at the absurdity.* CHRISTIE *attempts an imitative chuckle, but fails. He covers up with a slight cough.*

I mean, that's ridiculous, isn't it? You're not, are you?

CHRISTIE. Oh ay.

INSPECTOR. You're just a grubby rent payer.

CHRISTIE. Oh ay.

The INSPECTOR *holds out three fingers.*

INSPECTOR. Three weeks behind.

A pause.

In fact, after you left Ten Rillington Place, and before Constable Thomas picked you up on the embankment at two o'clock in the morning, the landlord came round and found, not only that you owe two weeks, but you had sublet the flat for the sum of seven pounds ten shillings in advance.

Sublet illegally. I'm not criticising you Reg. Not for that anyway. But you're no bigtime owner of property.

A pause.

CHRISTIE. Oh ay.

INSPECTOR. Still, be that as it may. Tiny isn't it?

A pause.

A tiny place.

CHRISTIE. It's a small house.

INSPECTOR. Cramped.

CHRISTIE. It's on the small side.

INSPECTOR. So you'd agree. It's cramped.

CHRISTIE. I said, it's a small house.

Suddenly the INSPECTOR *shouts.*

INSPECTOR. Oh ay. It's . . .

A pause.

Cramped all right.

INSPECTOR. You could say crammed.

CHRISTIE. You could say that.

INSPECTOR. Crammed with, eh, people?

CHRISTIE. There are a lot.

INSPECTOR. Why there's your Mrs, but then she's moved away hasn't she? Gone off? Still it's tiny and there's you downstairs. Poor old Mr Kitchener on the first floor. And on the top there's that young couple, the Evans's.

CHRISTIE. Browns.

INSPECTOR. Oh. Silly of me. Of course. The Browns were involved in that affair weren't they? Timothy Brown. Did his wife and little baby in.

CHRISTIE. No. Evans.

INSPECTOR. What?

CHRISTIE. Timothy Evans. Did his wife and little baby in.

The INSPECTOR *slaps his thigh.*

INSPECTOR. I am a stupid clot! Evans was the bloke not Brown.
Course you helped us a lot there, didn't you Reggie. Timothy
Evans did his wife and kid in, and stuck 'em in the washhouse
out the back of your property. You helped us a lot.

CHRISTIE. I did my bit.

INSPECTOR. You did.

CHRISTIE. I did my bit for public good.

INSPECTOR. And you're going to do your bit again Reginald.
Aren't you?

A pause.

CHRISTIE. I'll give what help's within my power.

The INSPECTOR *is delighted.*

INSPECTOR. You mean that?

CHRISTIE. Oh ay.

The INSPECTOR *is suddenly brisk.*

INSPECTOR. Good. First point. The house you rent is crammed
full not only of living, rent-paying tenants like yourself, but
crammed full of dead women.

A pause.

I say women loosely. Most of 'em far as the pathologists can
tell were tarts. The real dregs, and hardly a loss to humanity.
But women, tarts, ladies or bleeding duchesses, your small
house is stuffed to the roof with their remains.

A pause.

Now I don't want to get emotional. And I know that you are
not an emotional man. So there is no reason to get het up.
But I got to ask you this Reg. Can you help us with our
enquiries?

CHRISTIE *sits stock still on his chair for a second, then
shifts slightly.*

For example. The 22nd of June last year, a very hot day,
you were observed by a tenant to be sprinkling Jeyes' Fluid
in the passage. Between ourselves, man to man, couldn't
you stand the smell?

At once, CHRISTIE *half rises from his chair.*

CHRISTIE. I'm not going to sit here . . .

INSPECTOR. Oh you are. You are going to sit there.

CHRISTIE *sits. The* INSPECTOR *smiles.*

INSPECTOR. Remember, you are not an emotional man.

CHRISTIE. No. I don't like to let my feelings show.

INSPECTOR. Stiff upper lip!

The INSPECTOR *laughs.*

Everyone in the street says that of you, all your neighbours.
Mr Christie keeps a stiff upper lip. Keeps himself to himself.
Keeps . . . Neat.

A pause.

All right we'll forget about the Jeyes for the time being. Why
shouldn't a householder that is a rent-paying tenant keep
his place sanitary? Jeyes is just the thing in hot weather.
Clean and pungent, overriding any other odour. I'm not
unreasonable Reg. I'm not going off on an emotional tack.
Like accusing you of doing your Mrs in and burying her under
the floorboards in the front room. From where, by the way,
we dug her up the other day. I mean I'm not going off at a
tangent. I just don't know where to begin. But I wondered
if you could help.

A pause.

With a few details.

A pause.

Like why you killed those tarts.

A pause.

And did you fuck them before or after?

Blackout.

Scene Five

Lit by a camera flash bulb, CHRISTIE *rises, leans over the table and masturbates. On the tape women's voices call out, overlapping and laughing.*

TAPE. . . . Reggie.
  . . . Reggie Weggie.
  . . . Reggie No Dick.
  . . . Where is you Reggie?
  . . . What you doing Reggie?
  . . . It dirty Reggie?
  . . . It nasty?
  . . . Nasty little boy we going to get you.
  . . . Reginald! Stop that at once!
  . . . Going to get Reggie No Dick.
  . . . Reggie! Stop that nasty thing!
  . . . Going to cut off Reggie Weggie's Dicky Wick.

The lights are snapped up. CHRISTIE *whirls round, looking at the audience section by section, terrified. He sits down. By a series of gestures, he attempts to recover — he hitches his trousers, straightenes his tie, smoothes his lapels.*

Scene Six

The INSPECTOR *approaches* CHRISTIE, *holding out a glass phial.*

INSPECTOR. Know what this is? It intimately concerns you.

CHRISTIE. Oh ay.

INSPECTOR. It is your semen Reginald.

A pause.

The Christie family jewels. Hot stuff, eh Reg? You reckon that's hot stuff?

The INSPECTOR *steps into the garden, and shoves the phial under* CHRISTIE's *nose.*

Eh? Go on have a whiff. Don't mind me.

CHRISTIE *leans back, to avoid the phial. The* INSPECTOR *puts the phial on the table.*

Medical Science tells us there are millions of potential little Reginalds in that tube.

The INSPECTOR *shakes his head.*

What a waste. But you did not encourage them to come to fruition did you. The use you put your spunk to did not encourage birth.

CHRISTIE *mumbles, indistinctly.*

CHRISTIE. You're being bloody personal.

INSPECTOR. What you say Reg? Speak up.

CHRISTIE. You're being bloody personal.

INSPECTOR. Enunciate with clarity you fucking pervert.

CHRISTIE. Bloody personal!

CHRISTIE *puts his hand to his chest.*

Gas. Got load in First War.

INSPECTOR. What? What?

CHRISTIE. Got load of gas. 1918. Three years, couldn't speak.

INSPECTOR. Ah! Your war disability.

CHRISTIE. Honourably disabled.

CHRISTIE *breathes heavily.*

INSPECTOR. You sniveller. I dunno, it's disappointing. Why can't a mass murderer be just a bit diabolical? Why can't a pervert like you, already in the annals of nastiness, have fangs or something? Roll your eyes around. Sprout horns.

The INSPECTOR *kicks up the paper in a fury.*

Go on Reg, let's have a real bit of horror!

A pause. CHRISTIE *speaks weakly.*

CHRISTIE. I've overlooked my inhaler. Could you send round for it? Do you think? For my catarrh?

The INSPECTOR *shakes his head, saddened.*

INSPECTOR. And Madam Tussauds has been onto us all day for a plaster cast of your head.

CHRISTIE. My inhaler.

INSPECTOR. No you can't have your bloody inhaler!

CHRISTIE. I got my rights.

INSPECTOR That inhaler is the property of the Crown. We don't know what you been up to with it, do we.

CHRISTIE. I don't know what you're inferring.

INSPECTOR. Lots Reg. The whole filthy bundle I'm inferring.

CHRISTIE. If I don't have my inhaler, I'll come over with an attack.

The INSPECTOR *speaks confidentially.*

INSPECTOR. Don't threaten me.

A pause. The INSPECTOR *points at the phial.*

Forensics, Reg. It is all a matter of traces. The chalky soil from the flowerbed on the cat thief's boot. The tell-tale powder burn on the bank robber's sleeve. To the forensic scientist the criminal is always leaving his signature. It may be his finger prints. His dandruff. His spit, or his urine. Or, as in your case, his sperm.

A pause.

The dead tarts, Reg. They're full of your stuff. Science knows you fucked them all.

Scene Seven

CHRISTIE *and the* INSPECTOR *freeze. The* CONSTABLE *has been drinking at the back.*

CONSTABLE. Bloody hell!

The CONSTABLE *stumbles to the centre.*

Oh bloody hell. I'm bloody overwhelmed. Went home to my Mrs. You smell she said. Course I smelled, all day digging in his graveyard. Had three baths in a row. Disinfected me all over. Scrubbed me nails. Pumiced me palms. No good! Me Mrs could smell 'em. The dead women on me. I could not stand the look my very own and loved and cherished gave me. Went round the pub. Started to knock it back. And it all went round in my head. Him. In his kitchen he had a tin. Old Holborn 'baccy tin, of two ounce size. Know what he had in that tin? Pubic hairs, cut off the women he had. Bloody hell.

He cut off their pubic hairs and kept them in a tin. I tell you its all too . . .

The CONSTABLE *searches for the word.*

Deep for me.

The CONSTABLE *stumbles to the back, and kneels down by the* DOLL *on the stretcher.*

Scene Eight

INSPECTOR. Our pathologists conclude, the women were getting cold. You had 'em dead, didn't you.

CHRISTIE *stands violently, and knocks over the table and chair.*

INSPECTOR. Finally got to your bent have we? Touch of the necrophiliacs, eh?

At the same time the CONSTABLE *picks up the* DOLL *in his arms, and talks to her.*

CONSTABLE. Eh my love? What? What? I dunno.

INSPECTOR. Like your women drained of blood? Like your women cooled off? Don't work any other way for you, eh? Got to get 'em ready, hang 'em up stuck like a pig? If you weren't a well known anti-semite I'd say you were after a good kosher fuck.

CHRISTIE *faints, full length. He crawls feebly in the paper. The lights begin to fade.*

Tell me how you really like it. Love. I will not be shocked. I am a policeman of the realm. I am conversant with it all. The sinks and sewers of the minds of men and women. I spend my professional life in the General Public's shithouse. I am a father to your kind, Reg. Tell your father.

The light is almost gone.

Scene Nine

Red light. The INSPECTOR *goes to the back. The* CONSTABLE *comes forward with the* DOLL *in his arms circles the garden, showing her to the audience.*

CONSTABLE. Just a scrubber. Twenty-six. Tits a bit worn. The rest of her, a bit worn. A very ordinary bint. I wouldn't have minded a go. I mean, if she weren't a rotting corpse I'd have, perhaps, chanced my arm.

CHRISTIE *stands.*

CHRISTIE. NO ONE PLAYS THE FOOL WI' ME. SEE? NO MAN NO WOMAN. PLAYS THE FOOL WI' ME.

CHRISTIE *lifts a foot.*

See my plims?

CHRISTIE *steps out of the garden.*

No woman ever knows if I'm near or not. I pass like a ghost through Society. The petty criminal in his den, the tart in her red room. I come and go, a military looking gent. A good citizen, in plims.

CONSTABLE. She were only a common day fuck. That's all. Used, yeh, but a common . . .

He searches for the word.

Woman.

To CHRISTIE.

So what you have to go and do perversions for? She offer first? Or did you have to force your foul desire? And what she say when she first approached? She say . . .

The CONSTABLE *actor holds the* DOLL *before him, and works the arms and head for occasional gestures. He speaks the woman's part, in a falsetto voice, over the* DOLL's *shoulder.*

DOLL. Want a touch love?

A pause.

Want a touch love?

A pause.

Want a touch love?

CHRISTIE. No one touches me!

DOLL. Sorry I'm sure.

She turns away.

CHRISTIE. Eh up there.

She turns back.

DOLL. What?

CHRISTIE. Want to touch me do you?

DOLL. All the same to me love. Touch or not touch, if the price is right.

CHRISTIE. Bloody tarts! Coming up, touching you!

DOLL. All right, all right.

CHRISTIE. Want to get your hands on me don't you. Get your fingers. On. Want to poke me.

DOLL. I don't have to stand here and talk to you. There're too many queer fishes about nowadays. A girl's not safe. The Government should do something.

She turns away.

CHRISTIE. Eh up there.

She stops, and turns back.

DOLL. Do you don't you? Make up your bleeding mind.

CHRISTIE. See my plims?

DOLL. Very nice.

CHRISTIE. I creep about in them.

DOLL. I don't doubt it.

CHRISTIE. I come up unawares in them.

DOLL. Do you.

CHRISTIE. Then I pounce.

DOLL. That's not very nice, is it.

CHRISTIE. It ain't nice come to think of it. Come to think of it, it's . . . Nasty.

DOLL. It's very nasty.

CHRISTIE. Women bring out the nastiness in me.

DOLL. Do they.

CHRISTIE. They bring it out. And they love it, the stupid bitches. That's all they want. To be kicked about a bit. Be scared to shits. You scared to shits, girly?

DOLL. Cost you money to scare me.

CHRISTIE. How much?

DOLL. Two quid.

CHRISTIE. One pound ten.

DOLL. Thirty-five bob.

CHRISTIE. Thirty-five bob.

DOLL. I'm scared.

CHRISTIE. Ha!

CHRISTIE backs away, pointing at her.

Ha!

He holds out his police identification. She peers at it.

DOLL. Constable John Reginald Christie. You're a fucking dick.

CHRISTIE. Just a Special.

DOLL. Still a fucking dick.

CHRISTIE. Still very much a fucking dick.

DOLL. What a come on. You deliberately encouraged my soliciting, pretending you were a queer fish just to get a girl arrested.

CHRISTIE. I'm a respectable citizen girly. I was gassed in the First World War. Couldn't speak for three year. I served my country.

DOLL. An amateur policeman. Just my luck.

CHRISTIE. Watch your lip yer whore.

A pause.

DOLL. Well come on. Take my name. Take my address. Take me down the station for a good laugh with your friends.

A pause.

What you waiting for?

A pause.

Ruth Fuerst, 27, Ladbroke Grove. Twenty-six years old. I'm not wholly on the game. I would describe myself as an experienced amateur. I have prostitutes among my friends. I work as a nurse. I get bored a lot.

CHRISTIE. Do it for free.

A pause.

You don't want to be charged for soliciting.

DOLL. You making a proposition?

CHRISTIE. Little arrangement.

DOLL. Stone me. If I take my knickers down to you, you let me go?

CHRISTIE. Don't be coarse.

DOLL. I'll believe anything of the police force now.

CHRISTIE. You keep respectful.

DOLL. I do it, you let me go. I don't do it, I get charged for prostitution. That really takes the pip.

A pause.

Haven't got much choice, have I?

CHRISTIE. None.

DOLL. I think that I'm in your power.

The CHRISTIE *actor embraces the* DOLL. *He takes her arm, they walk round two sides of the garden.* CHRISTIE *steps into the garden, the* CONSTABLE *actor follows, with the* DOLL. CHRISTIE *goes to a corner and fiddles with a cup and saucer and a teapot.*

DOLL. What a filthy house.

CHRISTIE. It's clean enough.

DOLL. What's all this stuff?

CHRISTIE. It's clean I said! Spotless.

DOLL. All right.

CHRISTIE. There's no dirt here!

DOLL. All right, all right!

She speaks aside.

He is a queer fish. THOUGH I've had queer fish in my time, AND left 'em to swim away. If you get my meaning. Here we go.

The CONSTABLE *actor strips off the* DOLL's *clothes.*

'Ere. What you doing out there?

CHRISTIE. Making cup of tea.

DOLL. Highly romantic. Two lumps please.

CHRISTIE, *to himself.*

CHRISTIE. Two lumps eh? Two lumps eh?

DOLL. Could do with a cup of tea.

CHRISTIE, *cup and saucer in one hand teapot in the other, whirls on her.*

CHRISTIE. Who said you were getting a cup?

DOLL. Ooh la la. Sorry I spoke I'm sure.

CHRISTIE. Tea's for after. That's how I like it, after.

DOLL. Come on then. Let's get it over with.

Scene Ten

The INSPECTOR *comes forward.* CHRISTIE *puts his hands on the* DOLL. *He speaks to the* INSPECTOR.

CHRISTIE. I have something on my mind. It comes back to me in flashes. If it does come back, I will tell you, I truly will.

CHRISTIE *puts his hand between the* DOLL's *legs.*

CONSTABLE. Hello! I think he's off.

CHRISTIE. I don't remember what happened. But I must have gone haywire.

The INSPECTOR *hands* CHRISTIE *a short length of rope.* CHRISTIE *whips it round the* DOLL's *neck, and strangles her.*

CONSTABLE. Sir! He's off! He's well away!

And CHRISTIE *has gone down, still pulling the rope tight. The* CONSTABLE *ends up in the paper, under the* DOLL, CHRISTIE *on top of them both.* CHRISTIE *lets go the rope.*

CHRISTIE. The next thing I remember she was lying down, a rope
about her neck. I left her there and went into the front room.
I had a cup of tea, and I went to bed. I got up in the morning,
and washed and shaved. She still lay there. I had a cup of tea.
I pulled away a cupboard and gained access to a small alcove.
I knew it was there because a pipe burst in the frosty weather
and a plumber opened it up to mend the pipe.

CONSTABLE. This is getting out of hand. Right out.

CHRISTIE. I was in love with her.

Scene Eleven

The lights change from red to bright white. The CONSTABLE
throws the DOLL *and* CHRISTIE *off of him, and rises to
make his protest.*

CONSTABLE. That's not love.

INSPECTOR. Is to him.

CONSTABLE. Dead bodies?

CHRISTIE *takes up the* DOLL, *and carries her on his knees
to the other side of the garden, and buries her as best he can
in the newspaper.*

CHRISTIE. Took her out the back. Wrapped her up in old
newspaper. Buried her.

CONSTABLE. Love's the bleeding moon. And bleeding doves
cooing. And bleeding Frank Sinatra crooning. And holding
hands. And a lovely bunch of roses from the one whom you
admire. And a nice church ceremony, and the Mrs tearful eyed
at the photograph. We went to Clacton for our honeymoon,
my wife and me. The sea was gentle as a baby. The moon was
smoochy yellow. That were love. Not a corpse, in a dirty
garden.

During his speech, the INSPECTOR *sets the chair in the centre
of the garden, stands on it, and rigs a noose up through the
rafters.*

INSPECTOR. One bloke we nicked, had a thing about handbags.
Couldn't keep himself out of them. 'Nother bloke we nicked,
had a thing about pussycats. The handbag man we got for

shop lifting. The pussycat man we got for cruelty to animals. See Reg, you got to keep love in bounds. Else it gets criminal. And we can't have that, can we.

Standing on the chair, the INSPECTOR *bellows to all the audience.*

Society cannot allow the fucking of handbags. Pussycats. Dead women. What would happen if we all went right ahead, according to desire, fucking all? Bleeding anarchy Reg. Larceny, mutilation of animals, murder.

The police shout angrily at CHRISTIE, *who is still kneeling over the* DOLL's *grave.*

CONSTABLE. You filthy beast! You utter cad!

INSPECTOR. Bloody pervert!

CONSTABLE. Bloody pervert!

INSPECTOR. Go one better than us would you, eh? Eh? Defile English Womanhood?

CONSTABLE. Cast aspersions on my mother!

INSPECTOR. Cast aspersions would you!

The CONSTABLE, *all self control gone, grabs* CHRISTIE, *who's limp and barely whispers, and drags him up to the noose. The Police hang* CHRISTIE. CHRISTIE *falls into the paper, the noose still about his neck. A pause. The* INSPECTOR *steps down from the chair, straightens his uniform. Both policemen are shaken, shamefaced.*

INSPECTOR. That's that then.

CONSTABLE. Yes Sir.

INSPECTOR. Another crime solved.

CONSTABLE. A blow struck for married life.

INSPECTOR. Yes.

CONSTABLE. Yes.

The INSPECTOR *puts the chair upside down on the table, picks the table up, about to carry it off. He stops.*

INSPECTOR. Just . . . Clean up a bit. Someone else's garden now.

CONSTABLE. Sir.

INSPECTOR. Get on with it then.

CONSTABLE. Sir.

> *The* CONSTABLE *covers the body of* CHRISTIE *with the spade, slowly, smoothes the surface of the paper down, then looks around the audience, shamefaced, and slips away. End play.*

Gum and Goo

Gum & Goo was first performed by the Brighton Combination in January 1969, with Katya Benjamin, James Carter and Howard Brenton. Directed by Ruth Marks.

Performed many times throughout 1969 and 1970 by the Bradford University Theatre Group, with Michele Ryan, Greg Philo and Phil Emmanuel. Directed by Chris Parr.

(Their performance of this piece was very fine: I've used their names for the parts in the script. H.B.)

Performed by the Royal Shakespeare Company at the Open Space, London, at lunchtime in February 1971. Directed by Janet Henfrey.

Author's Note

Gum & Goo was written at the Brighton Combination in January of 1969. A Teachers Conference asked for a show. There were eight days to make something. We kicked ideas around for two days from a scene I'd written about a little girl down a hole. I wrote the script in the next two days. The remaining four days we rehearsed it.

The play was formed by thinking of whom it was being done for (the teachers), where (a gymnasium floor with two big lights and a possible blackout), and who was free to do it (two big blokes, James Carter and myself, and a girl, Katya Benjamin). Ruth Marks directed us.

So the play was 'tailor-made'. A response to an invitation to perform, with what was to hand — three actors, a few days, a budget of thirty shillings for a ball and three bicycle lamps.

H.B.

As the audience come in, GREG, PHIL *and* MICHELE *are playing touch-he, in a circle.*
The audience sit all around.
When they're all in, the game goes on for a while.
A plastic football's thrown into the circle.
They pick it up, throw and bounce it about, off the walls, on the ceiling, it's fun.
It stops being fun. The two boys begin to hog the ball.
Piggy in the middle starts. It's fair at first.
But MICHELE *gets stuck in the middle.*
GREG *and* PHIL *torment her, hide the ball behind their backs, hold it above her head. She goes on tiptoe to try and get it.*
Suddenly, GREG *throws the ball to* MICHELE.
Delighted, she throws the ball to PHIL, *to start the piggy game again.*
But the boys play dead, let the ball roll away.
She tries again to get them to play, but they just stand still.
She gives up, sad. Sits down, lets the ball roll away.
Stands up, turns away, sucks her thumb.

GREG. There's that goofy kid again. Goofy!

PHIL. Goofy goofy!

GREG. Goofy goofy!

> GREG *goes up to her.*
> *Pause.*
> *Then suddenly he lifts her skirt with his toe.*

GREG. She's got corrugated knickers on, 'cos she wets herself!

PHIL. Goofy goofy!

GREG. Goofy goofy!

> *A pause.*

GREG. 'Ere. I bet her Dad's a gorilla.

PHIL. I bet her Ma's a Ford Cortina.

GREG. Don't be stupid. A gorilla and a Ford Cortina can't have sex.

PHIL. Yeh, they can.

GREG. Can't.

PHIL. Can.

GREG. Can't.

PHIL. Can.

GREG. Where would the gorilla put it in then? That's what I'd like to know. Where would he put it in?

PHIL. In her petrol pump!

GREG. Up her exhaust!

PHIL. Smash right through her rear window!

GREG. You've got a dirty mind for a twelve-year-old.

PHIL. Yours in't bad, and you're eleven.

> *A pause.*
> *They stare at* MICHELE.

GREG. Eh, goof. Tell us what your Ma's like.

> *A pause.*
> *Then* MICHELE *goes down on her knees and mimes an igloo shape.*
> *The boys are nonplussed.*

GREG. Looks like an igloo.

> MICHELE *mimes a door.*

It is an igloo. That was the door.

> MICHELE *crawls through the 'door' and snuggles up.*

What do you make of that?

PHIL. Freak in her head, in't she? My Dad says they all should be put away, all them communists and freaks. My Dad says put them away.

GREG. 'Ere. You ever though what it's like to be a nut?

PHIL. If I were a nut?

GREG. If you were a nut, what would you do?

PHIL. I'd do . . .

> *Thinks. Then he gets excited.*

Women in! With a knife!

PHIL *mimes raising a knife and stabbing.*
He lurches about, attempting a horror face and walk.

GREG. What you doing?

PHIL. I'm doing women in with a knife, 'cos I'm DOCTOR CRIPPEN.

He stabs away.

GREG. You don't look like Doctor Crippen to me.

PHIL. I'm going to Doctor Crippen you in your gut.

PHIL *makes a lunge at* GREG. *They fight, roll over on the floor, kicking and struggling. Then they roll apart, tired of the game.*

You know what Doctor Crippen did? When he'd done 'em in, he put 'em in a bath, nude. And all the blood SPURTED out in the water. Then he bottled the bathwater and drank it on Sundays.

GREG. That weren't Crippen.

PHIL. That were!

GREG. It weren't! It were Haigh.

PHIL. It were Crippen and I read it in a book called Crime does not Pay.

GREG. Anyway, Crippen, Haigh, they were nothing to Adolf Hitler.

MICHELE *moans quietly.*

PHIL. My Dad says, Hitler was a man terribly wronged.

GREG. My Dad says Hitler was the biggest bad man who ever lived. And Winston Churchill got him: BANG.

MICHELE's *moaning grows.*

Winston Churchill stood on the cliffs of Dover in his battle-dress and he made this speech 'bout filling up the hole with the English dead. Then Winston Churchill took out this great big gun and he SMASHED Adolf Hitler.

MICHELE's *moaning becomes a scream.*

PHIL. Eh. Look at her.

MICHELE *begins to rock backward and forward, moaning. The boys are panicky.*

GREG. She's goofy.

They shout at her.

PHIL. Oy! Iron knickers!

GREG. Goofy!

MICHELE's *screams and rocking become horrible, then
suddenly stop.
She's dead still, eyes closed.
A pause.*

I think she's dead. You think she's dead? She's dead.

PHIL. Na, she's fainsy. Oy kid!

Nothing from MICHELE.

GREG. She's dead.

GREG *and* PHIL *stare at each other.
Blackout.
In the blackout, at once.* GREG *speaks the following deadpan,
that is as fact, and not poetry.* PHIL *whispers the words almost
simultaneously, but not quite — a fraction after.*

The dark inside.
The light inside the dark inside.
The beautiful lands inside.
The lovely ladies in the fields inside.
The silver children and the animals at play inside.
The snows, and Christmas-is-forever inside.

MICHELE, *at once, with a cutting, official doctorish voice.*

MICHELE. In the extreme condition, the child's senses are totally
dislocated. Fire is cold, cold burns. Words screech. Animate
objects are stone. The child walks on another planet, converses
with beings not conceived of by the natural world.

And at once, GREG *and* PHIL *switch hand lamps on.
NB: At the Brighton Combination, we had these set on the
floor. That was a bit ugly, we had to find them in the blackout.
In the production by the Bradford Theatre Group and the
RSC they carried the lamps in their pockets.* GREG *and* PHIL
*as Gum & Goo. Grins. They overlap their cues to each other,
their words tumble over each other.*

GREG. Mary.

PHIL. Mary.

GREG. Mary Mary Mary.

PHIL. Mary had-a-little-lamb Mary.

Lamps onto MICHELE, *who stares straight ahead.*

MICHELE. Who you?

GREG. I Gum Gum.

PHIL. I Goo Goo.

GREG. He Goo Goo.

PHIL. He Gum Gum.

Lamps on MICHELE.

MICHELE. What you?

Lamps on GREG *and* PHIL.

GREG. We Gremlins, Mary.

Lamps on MICHELE.

MICHELE. Grem-lins.

Lamps on GREG *and* PHIL.

GREG. He Gremlin Goo, I Gremlin Gum.

GREG *and* PHIL *nod frantically, then lamps on* MICHELE.

MICHELE. You good, or you bad?

Lamps back on GREG *and* PHIL.

GREG. We good Mary. In't we Goo?

PHIL. Yeh, we good. Very very good.

GREG. We very very very good.

GREG *and* PHIL *nod frantically.*

Not bad.

GREG *and* PHIL *shake their heads.*

PHIL. We not bad.

GREG. We not ever bad. 'Cos we're good.

GREG *and* PHIL *nod.*

We your friends Mary.

GREG. You want us be your friends?

Lamps on MICHELE.

MICHELE. You . . . My . . . Friends?

Lamps on GREG *and* PHIL.

GREG. We your friends. You don't need other friends, when you got Gum and Goo.

PHIL. Gum and Goo, friends with you.

GREG. Gum and Goo do what you want to do, Mary. Mary, what you want to do?

Lamps onto MICHELE.

MICHELE. Where the lovely ladies are and. Go there. It's Christmas. And where the animals are. And where it's magic all day and. And.

A pause.
The lamps stay on MICHELE.

GREG. You go there Mary.

PHIL. You go there.

MICHEEE. Go now?

GREG. Not now Mary.

PHIL. Not now Mary.

GREG. You go home now Mary.

MICHELE. I want to play.

GREG. We play. But not now.

PHIL. Go home Mary.

GREG. Go home and have your tea. And don't tell.

PHIL. Don't tell.

GREG. Don't tell, on Gum and Goo.

Lamps out.

MICHELE. Gum. Goo.

Lights up. GREG *and* PHIL *are standing.*
MICHELE *stands up.*

Sometimes I go funny, and I fall down. And.

A pause.

But then I stand up. An' I go home for tea.

A street scene.
GREG as a business man, hailing a taxi.
PHIL as a policeman, directing traffic.
Then as men in the street, walking about turning corners.

GREG. Taxi!

A pause. GREG watches a taxi passing him, hails one coming the other way.

Taxi!

GREG and PHIL move toward each other, in a square figure.
They recognize each other, smile, shake hands.
They at once move on, blank faced.
Walk to other corner of the square, where PHIL bumps GREG on the shoulder and walks straight on.
GREG turns on him in an ugly way.
Then PHIL stops still.
GREG walks up and down, 'waiting for a bus', looking at his watch.

MICHELE. The streets in our town are funny an' I get lost. An' I get scared.

Goes up to PHIL.

'Scuse me mister, can you tell me where a toilet is?

PHIL moves on, then freezes.
MICHELE goes up to GREG.

'Scuse me mister, can you tell me where a toilet is?

GREG ignores her, still waiting, then freezes.

An' when I'm scared I think. I think I'll burn the whole world down. That's what I think. I'll burn the houses down and burn the mums and dads down. I'll burn my mum and dad down. Specially my mum. I'd like to see my mum's hair burn and hear her scream. She screamed once when I threw the iron at her. It made a funny mark on her face. I'd like to see her silly legs up burning and her knickers turning black. And when all the world was burnt I'd. I'd. BE HAPPY.

PHIL, as the mother, mimes taking an apron down, tying it round her waist, smoothing her hair. Comes into the centre, and starts kitchen work.

GREG *as the father, in another room, reading a newspaper.
The mother's soppy.*

MICHELE. Mummy Mummy.

PHIL. Not now Mary.

A pause.
MICHELE *sulks, calculating.*

MICHELE. YOUR HAIR'S ON FIRE.

PHIL. WHAT?

She clutches her hair. Then arranges it, tired, back to work.

Oh Mary, you're telling lies again.

MICHELE. It was.

A pause.
MICHELE *sulks, calculating.*

MICHELE. LOOK, A RAT.

PHIL. AHH. WHERE?

MICHELE. UNDER THE COOKER.

PHIL. AHH.

A pause.
Mother on her toes.
She calms down.

Oh Mary, that was another lie, I don't know what makes you
tell them. You mustn't tell lies.

She goes back to work.

MICHELE. What's for tea?

PHIL. It's bread and butter, and that nice raspberry jam you like
I got some in specially.

MICHELE. I bet it's rat. I bet it's rat for tea. Rat on toast.

PHIL. Mary, what a wicked thing to say to your mother.

MICHELE. Rat rat rat! You give me rat for tea, you ratbag.

PHIL. Mary!

MICHELE *jumping up and down.*

MICHELE. Ratbag ratbag ratbag.

PHIL *slaps* MICHELE's *face.*
MICHELE *stops jumping, stares, then howls.*
PHIL *at once mortified.*
MICHELE *puts all the agony on, falls down on the floor, howling.*
PHIL *leans over, trying to get her to stand up.*

PHIL. Don't cry, Mary, I'll get you ice-cream for tea. Mary, don't cry. Pink and green ice-cream, you like that. Don't cry Mary. Strawberry ripple ice-cream Mary . . .

MICHELE *grabs her mother's hair.*

Mary Mary Mary let go my hair!

GREG *comes in as the father.*

GREG. Mary! Let go your mother's hair at once!

MICHELE *does so, and turns on her father.*

MICHELE. Daddy rat, the biggest rat of all.

She hits her father in the balls.

GREG. OOOOH.

He doubles up.

MICHELE. I'm going out to play, and I hope you BURN.

MICHELE *turns away.*
PHIL *as mother, clutching hair.*
GREG *as father, clutching crotch.*

PHIL. What did we do to deserve such a child?

GREG. Don't distress yourself, my love. We must have patience.

PHIL. Patience.

GREG. Patience.

PHIL. But what did we do, and where did she get those thoughts?

They freeze in their contorted positions, as MICHELE *does her speech.*

MICHELE. I was playing with my mum, and I got hold of her head, and it roll off. Under the table. And I run down the garden. And my mum's head it roll after me. And I go in the shed. And I shut the shed and. My Mum's head it bump against the door bump bump bump. And say let me in Mary, Mary let me in.

MICHELE *draws the igloo, and goes into it.*
PHIL *crouches down at the side of the playing area, out of it
for the moment.*
GREG *goes into an old man, going round the circle working
in a limp, a drag of the limping leg, swinging of an arm, cough,
spit and stoop. Stops by* MICHELE.

GREG. Oy Miss. You got a penny on you?

MICHELE. Why? You want to go to the toilet?

GREG. Maybe I do, and maybe I don't.

GREG's *old man gets a bag of sweets out of his coat, mimed.*

MICHELE. You a dirty old man? You got some sweeties?

GREG. Have a sweetie.

MICHELE. You are a dirty old man. You'll be my very own
dirty old man.

MICHELE *goes to take a sweet, but* GREG *suddenly withdraws the bag.*

GREG. I was in the war. I made the dead. You alive, or dead?

MICHELE. ImmmmmmmmmDEAD.

GREG. Wa?

MICHELE. I'm a ghost. Waaa Waaa.

GREG *turns away.*

Oy Mister, don't go away. Tell me 'bout the dead.

GREG. Wa?

MICHELE. I saw a film about the dead. It were Dracula. I got
into see it through the exit door. It were *Dracula Has Risen
from the Grave.* There were lots of blood.

GREG *jerks and begins to turn round.*

Dracula got stuck on this cross right through his heart. That
were good. An' he bit a lovely lady in the neck. That were
very good.

Change.

But half-way through the film I went funny.

GREG. The dead lie with rotting eyes. And the Lord calls, and they rise up. Have a sweetie.

MICHELE *takes one.*
GREG, *at once.*

I got a place.

MICHELE. What, a secret place?

GREG. Out there.

GREG *gestures.*

MICHELE. Out on the rocks? It's creepy there.

GREG. There.

MICHELE. It your Dracula tomb?

MICHELE *stands.*

Let's go there mister, go there and play.

GREG. Wa?

GREG *takes her by the hand. They go along together.*
MICHELE *saying 'We play biting lovely ladies' necks an'
crosses through your heart . . .' etc.*
PHIL *stands. As policeman. Walks towards them.*

PHIL. Hello hello hello.

MICHELE. Look out, it's a copper.

PHIL. Sweeties, is it?

GREG. Wa?

PHIL *grabs* GREG's *arm, twists it.* GREG's *old man goes down.*

PHIL. Child fingerer are you? Child fingerer, eh? Scum you are.
Scum on the milk of society.

MICHELE. Let him go, copper.

PHIL. Finger kids eh, finger kids eh?

GREG. Ahh!

MICHELE. Let him go, let him go.

PHIL. It's all right, my love, you're safe now.

MICHELE. Let him go, he's my dirty old man not yours. You
fucking copper.

MICHELE *pummels the policeman's back.*

PHIL. 'Ere! You little cow. I'll deal with you later.

MICHELE. He's mine. We was going to play Dracula then you came, you fucking copper. My dirty old man and me, we were gonna bite the lovely ladies in the neck. And it would snow, and then you come along you FUCKING COPPER.

MICHELE stamps her foot, and turns away.

PHIL. She's run off, and I've not got her name and address. But I still got you. You're a catch, sonny boy. We've not had a child fingerer down the station for weeks. It'll be drinks all round on the Inspector tonight!

PHIL and GREG freeze, as the copper twisting the arm of the old man.

MICHELE. All go away. Way way way. All go. Dirty old man, don't go.

Blackout.
Gum & Goo again.

GREG. Mary.

PHIL. Mary.

Lamps on GREG and PHIL.

GREG. Gum not go.

PHIL. Goo not go.

GREG. We stay and play with you.

Lamps on MICHELE.

MICHELE. Play now. You play now.

MICHELE stamps her foot.
Lamps on GREG and PHIL.

GREG. Not here.

PHIL. Not here Mary.

GREG. Out there.

PHIL. Out there.

GREG. Out the rocks Mary.

PHIL. We play out there.

Lamps on MICHELE.

MICHELE. But I not got my old man. And there big boys out the rocks. It scary. There . . . Holes out there. I not go out the rocks if I not got my old man.

The lamps remain on her.

GREG. But you got Gum.

PHIL. You got Goo.

GREG. We with you alway.

PHIL. Gum and Goo alway with you.

They're suddenly nasty to her.

GREG. Go there!

PHIL. Go there!

Sweetly.

GREG. Mary.

PHIL. Mary.

GREG. See ya.

Lamps out.

MICHELE. See ya Gum. See ya Goo.

At once lights up, GREG *and* PHIL *as the boys, straight into it . . .*

PHIL. I been reading this book 'bout Al Capone. 'Bout how he had this bullet proof limousine. And 'bout how he slayed hundreds. Hnnnnnnnnnnnnn.

GREG. Al Capone was nothing.

PHIL. Al Capone was not nothing. He was the biggest slob America has known and he slayed hundreds.

GREG. He was useless.

PHIL. He was tough.

GREG. He was a useless criminal.

A pause.

And anyway, Superman smashed him.

PHIL. Superman!

GREG. Superman smashed Al Capone with his super powers.

PHIL. You don't believe in Superman.

GREG. What if I do?

PHIL. Superman's for kids.

GREG. We're kids.

PHIL. But Superman. I bet you believe in Batman too.

GREG. Well?

PHIL. How stupid. How . . .

> *Mispronounces.*

Unutterably stupid. My Dad says them mags are . . .

> *Mispronounces.*

Unutterably stupid.

GREG. I seen you reading them.

PHIL. Where?

GREG. In the bog at school.

PHIL. That weren't Superman. That were Doctor Death. Doctor Death would crush Superman any day.

GREG. Wouldn't.

PHIL. Would.

GREG. Wouldn't.

PHIL. Would. Anyway, if Superman did crush Dr Death the RED SKULL would have revenge, 'cos of his invincibly evil brain.

GREG. Rubber man would crush the Red Skull anyday.

PHIL. Rubber Man? He's just a wet bit of elastic.

GREG. He's not! He's the Great Stretcho. He can knock a bad man out half a mile away 'cos his arm's like a rubber band. It shoots out with his mighty fist at the end of it, POW.

PHIL. POW.

GREG. POW.

PHIL. POW.

GREG. Then Captain America would sweep in with his mighty shield of freedom and ZAP all in sight. ZAP!

PHIL. ZAP!

GREG. ZAP!

PHIL. ZAP!

GREG. Be great to be a super hero.

PHIL. Be great to be a super villain.

GREG. It's getting dark.

PHIL. Yeh.

A slight pause.

GREG. Super villains get powed and zapped all the time.

PHIL. I'd not be. Soon as Superman and that lot came on the scene, I'd be off. Probably to Majorca with the great train robbers.

GREG. You couldn't escape the forces of good.

PHIL. Na?

GREG. Na.

PHIL. Bet I could.

GREG. It's really dark.

A pause.

PHIL. Not going, are you?

GREG. I just said it's dark.

PHIL. You scared?

GREG. You know what they say 'bout the rocks?

PHIL. What, ghosties?

PHIL *snorts.*
MICHELE *comes forward.*

GREG. It's the freak. Maybe the freaks come up here at night.

PHIL. What, and have it off with the ghosties?

To MICHELE.

Hello freak. What you doing up here? Little kids should not come up here in the darkies.

MICHELE. Play.

PHIL. What?

MICHELE. Want to. Play.

GREG. Freakie, freakie . . .

PHIL. Cut it out.

To MICHELE.

You want to play? What you want to play? I'm not going to hurt you kid. What you want to play?

MICHELE, *suddenly.*

MICHELE. I wanna play TOMBS. An' DEAD MEN. An' BITING NECKS. An' KICKING MY MUM'S HEAD.

Innocently.

You play with me?

PHIL, *nonplussed.*

PHIL. Yeh. Well. What do you reckon?

GREG. Yeh. Well. Could have a game or two.

MICHELE. I wanna play rotting eyes an' the dead rising up.

A pause.

GREG. Let's push off.

PHIL. No we're going to play. With the kid. We'll play with you kid, but the kind of games little kids should play. Like cowboys and Indians. Right? There's one thing though, kid. You're the Indian, right? And we're the cowboys, right? Bang. Bang.

GREG *stands awkwardly by.*

Come on!

Together they go bang bang and pistol firing noises near MICHELE.
But there's nothing from her, she just stands there.

Oy kid. Indians —

Hand to his mouth.

Go oyoyoyoyoyoyoyoyoyoyoyoyoyoyoyoy. Go oyoyoyoyoyoyoy.

MICHELE *makes the movement to her mouth, but silently.*

GREG. Let's push off.

PHIL *is incensed at her.*

PHIL. Oyoyoyoyoyoyoyoyoyoyoyoy.

PHIL gets GREG to join in. They do an Indian dance round her, then bang bang as cowboys. PHIL grabs her from behind.

PHIL. We got you Indian! We got you Indian! We got the dirty little Indian savage!

GREG. Yeh we got the Indian!

PHIL. Dirty Indian savage, you're our prisoner now!

A pause. Both breathless, excited.

Let's put our prisoner down that hole.

GREG. What?

PHIL. She's our prisoner! Put her down that hole!

PHIL drags her aside roughly, shoves her down the hole, shouts down at her.
Do this by having MICHELE 'down the hole' to one side, looking up, and GREG and PHIL looking down at the floor to one side of her.

You go down that hole you dirty dirty Indian.

He's hysterical, near tears.

And don't talk about the dead.

A pause.
Then GREG, tentatively.

GREG. She in't saying anything.

A pause.

You oughtn't to have put her down there.

PHIL. It was only a game.

A pause.

Kid. Game's over.

They look at each other.

GREG. You oughtn't to have.

PHIL. Kid.

GREG. Kid.

PHIL. Kid.

GREG. Kid.

PHIL. Kid.

A pause.

I got to go home now.

A pause.

Oy, kid. You all right down that hole?

GREG *and* PHIL *look at each other, then turn and run.*
Blackout as they're running.
A SECTION OF EFFECTS:
In the blackout, in their own words for a few sentences each,
GREG, MICHELE *and* PHIL *each tell what they thought*
Heaven was like when they were children.
A pause.
Then MICHELE *switches on a handlamp, moves it round the*
ceiling, begins a wail.
GREG *and* PHIL *come in, switching lights on, playing them*
round the ceiling, the 'wailing' has a canon effect. Experiment
showed that using a common sound, 'M', then each taking
a word, Mary/Margarine/Miranda, and sliding over the vowel
sounds in your word, made the desired effect.
This builds up. When MICHELE *goes into a scream, cut it.*
And snap the lamps out.
A pause.
Then MICHELE *switches her lamp on, shining it up into her*
own face. She looks up.
GREG, *as the father, switches his light on the ground, going*
all over the place.
PHIL, *as the Police Inspector, shines his on the ground too,*
but his search is methodical.

GREG. She ran out of the house.

PHIL. Oh yes sir.

GREG. Ran out.

A pause. They're looking on the ground . . .

Mary! Mary!

PHIL. That won't do much good sir. Why don't you go and have
a nice cup of tea.

GREG. You will find her.

PHIL. Oh we'll find her.

GREG. Inspector, over here!

A pause.

No. Inspector, over here!

A pause.

No.

PHIL. Let us handle it sir. We're used to it. Kids go down, in and up anything. We handle it.

A pause.

GREG. Mary's a difficult girl.

PHIL. They can be difficult.

GREG. Wilful.

PHIL. They can be wilful.

GREG. Not bad.

PHIL. No, not necessarily bad sir.

GREG. She has thoughts.

PHIL. They do have thoughts sir. You try and stop kids having thoughts, but they go right on and have them.

GREG. I don't know where they come from.

PHIL. That would be 'The age we live in', sir. Constable! Give those dogs fresh scent. You were saying, sir?

GREG. I was saying. What was I saying?

PHIL. I see them all. All the bad bits. The indecencies. We had one up here not long ago, an indecency.

GREG. Why don't you fill this place in?

PHIL. Ancient monument sir. Preservation Order.

GREG. But it's dangerous!

PHIL. Still ancient. Still a monument.

GREG. Mary! Mary!

PHIL. All right sir. Here she is.

Their lamps together on one spot, MICHELE *continuing to look up.*
She's not dead — worse, she's silent.

GREG. Mary.

PHIL. Mary.

GREG. Mary.

PHIL. Mary.

GREG. Mary.

PHIL. Mary.

GREG. Mary.

> GREG *and* PHIL *put their lamps out.* MICHELE *still looking up for a few seconds, then she puts her lamp out.*
> *End play.*

Heads

Heads was first presented by the University of Bradford Drama Group in June 1969 with the following cast:

MEGAN	Michele Ryan
ROCK	Phillip Emmanuel
BRIAN	Greg Philo

Directed by Chris Parr
Stage Manager Jo Stell

It was subsequently presented by Inter-Action at the Ambiance-In-Exile Lunch Hour Theatre Club, London, on 2 March 1970 with the following cast:

MEGAN	Frances Tomelty
ROCK	Christopher Martin
BRIAN	Michael Feast

Directed by Roland Rees
Stage Manager Roy Preston
Lighting by Nick Garnet

MICHELE, GREG *and* PHIL *in a circle.* PHIL *begins to limber up.* GREG *is reading a book.* MICHELE *stands aside, sexily.*

PHIL. Rock is my name and that sums up my body. Rock hard. Hup!

PHIL exercises.

Women have remarked before on my body. One woman said to me, Rock you're a symphony of gristle. Said she heard music everytime I flexed myself. Hup!

PHIL exercises.

GREG. I've always been rather . . .

GREG twitches.

Bright. When I was five, I performed the world's first heart transplant. On my Noddy. I got the heart from Big Ears. Of course it wasn't really a heart, just . . .

GREG twitches.

Stuffing.

MICHELE. Those are my two men, and I love them both for their various attributes. There a beautiful body, there a beautiful brain.

PHIL. I can't read much. Can't read at all, actually. Not that I got anything against books. I first showed my strength on a book. I was five years old at Sunday School and I tore up the Holy Bible, just like that. Hup!

PHIL exercises, then stops, and speaks reverently.

Course I did not know it was God's Word. Or any other word. A word to me is just a blur. The Holy Bible, The North Eastern Railway Time Table, The Thoughts of Chairman Mao Tse Tung. All a blur, to me.

Sadly.

Sometimes I wish I could read the little bastards, read the little blurs. La-dies, Gent-le-men.

Fiercely.

But I don't care. I don't need to read. I got my body and I'm happy. Hup!

PHIL *exercises.*

GREG. At school they called me boffin. They also called me The Mekon. They also called me Weed. And . . .

GREG *twitches.*

Twiggy. I was not popular. In gym periods when I took off my shirt they all cried Boneyard! Then I was exempted from gym and games, because of my asthma.

Bitterly.

Muscles are for cattle, who end as meat. It's not true all girls admire is muscular development. You don't need to twiddle your biceps when you've got a lively mind for girls to love.

MICHELE *goes up to* PHIL.

MICHELE. Hello Rock.

PHIL. Hello Fruitcake.

MICHELE. How are you Rock.

PHIL. Bulging my love. Have a feel.

PHIL *offers his biceps.* MICHELE *is shocked.*

MICHELE. Rock!

PHIL. Go on. You know you love that rippling sensation.

MICHELE. That's all you think of. Body body.

A pause. PHIL *flexes his biceps a few times, then speaks excitedly.*

PHIL. Crumpet.

MICHELE. What.

PHIL. They've come!

MICHELE. What have come?

PHIL. In the post this morning.

MICHELE. What, for crying out loud?

PHIL. My Mr Universe Big B Briefs.

MICHELE. Your what?

PHIL. My Mr Universe Big B Briefs.

MICHELE. Oh Rock, you've not replied to an advert on the back of the Radio Times, again.

PHIL. I've got them on underneath. Want a butchers?

MICHELE. No I do not want a butchers.

PHIL. What's the matter Crumpet? They show me off a treat.

MICHELE. I don't doubt it.

PHIL. They're as worn by Mr Universe himself. Make a great deal of sense out of my stance. Bags of lift.

MICHELE. Oh Rock, I wish you'd give up Physical Culture.

PHIL. Give up Physical Culture? You don't know what you're saying. I'd go flabby. Don't want me flabby do you? Not with a name like Rock.

MICHELE. I don't care.

PHIL. You don't care if I run to fat?

MICHELE. I don't. It's you I love, not your body.

PHIL. But I am my body.

MICHELE. You're rock.

PHIL. That's right. Rock's body.

MICHELE. Body body body. What about your head?

PHIL. My head? I got good neck muscles. Bulge a treat when I grit my teeth.

PHIL *grits his teeth.*

Have a feel.

MICHELE. I don't want to feel your muscles anymore. It's disgusting. You're always asking me to feel your muscles.

PHIL *is crestfallen.*

PHIL. You used to say they made you tingle.

MICHELE. What about your mind?

A pause.

PHIL. My what?

MICHELE. Your mind. Your thoughts.

PHIL. Yeh. Well.

MICHELE. What about poetry?

PHIL. Yeh.

PHIL *frowns.*

MICHELE. Intellectual pursuits. The discussion of international affairs. Bartok's String Quartets.

PHIL. You getting at me?

MICHELE. Your thoughts Rock. What do you think?

PHIL. What do I think?

MICHELE. What do you think?

PHIL. I think . . . How good it is. Yeh. When I've had a stiff work out, and have a shower, I think how good that is. Yeh.

A pause.

You are getting at me. Don't get at me, Fruitcake. I don't like being got at. I lose control. I don't want to lose control with you, you're nice. So don't get at me.

MICHELE. You great thick ha'p'orth. I'm sick of the smell of body oil. Sick of flesh flesh flesh.

PHIL. I'm sorry.

MICHELE *backs away.*

MICHELE. It's not all body, you know.

PHIL. Not all body? What else is there then? Other? What else, other than body?

PHIL *looks at his hands.*

Bone and gristle, that's you. Eight pints of blood. Millions of little nerves, hundreds of muscles in constant play. That's your body and that's you. All the rest is . . .

PHIL *makes a gesture of disgust.*

Talk.

MICHELE *goes up to* GREG.

MICHELE. Hello Brian.

GREG. Oh. Hello there.

MICHELE. How are you Brian.

GREG. Brushing up my vocabulary. Ask me a word.

MICHELE. Um. Palindrome?

GREG. Noun. Word, line, etc., that reads back and forwards, e.g. MADAM. Greek, meaning palin, again, psao, rub, dromos, run.

MICHELE. Um. Osmosis?

GREG. Neuter noun. Tendency of fluids, separated by membrane or other porous substance, to percolate and mix.

MICHELE. Give me a kiss.

> MICHELE *closes her eyes.* GREG *is embarassed.*

GREG. Noun. Caress with lips. In billiards impact between moving balls. Verb transitive. Touch with the lips.

> GREG *goes to kiss her, but retreats, and continues desperately.*

Kiss hands, sovereign's hand on appointment as minister. Kiss the dust, yield, abject submission, drop dead. Kiss the rod, accept submission submissively. Kiss-in-the-ring, a game. Kissing-crust, soft crust where loaf has touched another in baking. Kissing-gate, hung in U or V shaped enclosure. Don't do that!

MICHELE. Do what?

GREG. Pucker up your mouth.

MICHELE. Sometimes Brian, I wonder if you're frigid.

> GREG *with self-loathing.*

GREG. Adverb. Cold. Lacking ardour. Formal. Forced. Dull.

MICHELE. Sometimes I look at you reading poetry with your legs crossed and think 'he's not natural'.

GREG. Not natural?

MICHELE. Unhealthy.

GREG. Ah!

MICHELE. What do you mean Ah!

GREG. Big cocks.

MICHELE. Brian!

GREG. I thought you loved a lively mind. But it's big cocks in the end. That's what it comes down to, in the end. Length.

MICHELE. You've got a morbid mind, that's what.

GREG. If you met Socrates you'd not ask him the secret of the Universe. You'd ask him how big a cock he had.

MICHELE. And who was Socrates?

GREG. A fat old man.

MICHELE. I hate fat old men.

GREG. He was a monumental intellect!

MICHELE. I don't care. He was a fat old man and no doubt dirty too.

GREG. Actually he was homosexual.

MICHELE. There you are. That's where thinking gets you. Going against nature.

MICHELE *stamps her foot, and turns away. A pause, then* GREG, *shyly.*

GREG. How about a Violin Sonata.

A pause.

A Harpsichord Concerto.

MICHELE. Go away, you're queer.

MICHELE *turns her back on both of them.* PHIL *goes up to* GREG.

PHIL. Tough, eh mate?

GREG. What?

PHIL. Tough, when you've got bags of what they don't want.

GREG. Yes.

PHIL. I wish the brain didn't count.

GREG. I wish the body didn't count.

PHIL. I wish I were all animal.

GREG. I wish I were all intellect.

PHIL. I'd be free.

GREG. I'd be free.

PHIL. I'd be a horse. An Arabian steed of shiny flank, galloping over the desert. No thoughts just run run run in a world of sky and sand.

GREG. I'd be a brain. Only a brain. Suspended in jelly in a metal box. I'd have a loudspeaker on top of the box, to broadcast my thoughts. I'd be quite still, and just think.

PHIL. You wouldn't get around at all?

GREG. Maybe I'd have little wheels.

MICHELE *aside*.

MICHELE. All a girl wants is a husband, that's all. A good male body, strong enough, no TB, sexy enough. Brains up to a point, to work out the mortgage and the hire purchase. Don't want a Samson pulling buildings apart, don't want an Einstein living in the fourth dimension.

PHIL. If you were a brain, trundling round on wheels, what about women?

GREG. What about them?

PHIL. Be a bit difficult wouldn't it?

GREG. I don't see why.

PHIL. Difficult, having it off.

GREG. I see what you mean.

A pause.

We wouldn't.

PHIL. Oh.

MICHELE. Megan, my Ma said, Megan, beware of extremes and the men who go to them. Extremes bring Bailiff and Constable to the door.

PHIL. You'd not have it off at all?

GREG. Not exactly.

PHIL. No.

PHIL *frowns*.

Not exactly.

GREG. It would be a meeting of minds. We'd park next to each other and . . . Exchange information. Sort of caress each other's nerve ends.

PHIL *shakes his head.*

PHIL. Be a horse mate.

MICHELE. Megan, my Ma said, Megan, a man is a soggy bit of putty. You mould him to what you will. The woman makes the man, Megan. But Ma, I said, they told us in Sunday School the woman came from the rib. That's all propaganda she said, trumped up by males. Genesis was written by a man. Remember Megan, in the Old Religion God was a woman.

A pause. Then MICHELE, *with formality.*

These are my two men, and I love them both for their various attributes. What a pity what a joke, that they are made so extremely. What a pity what a joke, that that brain and that body
are not moulded in one
wholly normally whole
and lovely
man.

MICHELE *points slowly from* PHIL's *head to* GREG's, *from* GREG's *head to* PHIL's, *and thinks. Then snaps her fingers.*

MICHELE. What I need's an axe, and glue.

Blackout. A tape, 'Here comes a chopper to chop off your head . . .', chopping sounds, and screams. The screams continue for one minute. Lights up. Silence. GREG *and* PHIL *have changed clothes, and are back to back in the centre of the circle.* PHIL *is Rock's head on Brian's body.* MICHELE *stands aside, her arms are covered with tomato ketchup, in one hand she holds an axe, in the other a big tube of glue.*

Note. *Dear* GREG *and* PHIL. *Don't set yourself too much with this scene. Just follow the routine. Don't scream indiscriminately. 'Wha' means 'What?' Its a dialogue, question and answer between the two mutilations.*

GREG. Wha?

PHIL *starts at the sound, and jerks his head to one side.*

Wha?

PHIL. Wha?

A pause. They both stagger forward a few steps. The calls to each other get loud, then very loud.

GREG. Wha?

PHIL. Wha?

A pause.

GREG. Wha!

PHIL. Wha?

GREG. WHA?

A pause.

GREG. WHA?

PHIL. WHA?

GREG. WHA?

PHIL. WHA?

GREG. WHA?

PHIL. WHA?

GREG. WHA?

PHIL. WHA?

GREG. WHA?

A pause. A count of three. PHIL and GREG whirl round and stare at each other. A pause. Jerkily, they look down each other's body, to the feet. A pause. They jerk their heads up again, and stare. A pause. They each turn their attention to themselves. Then PHIL, as the weak head now on the weak body, crouches down with a little whimper. GREG, as the strong head now on the strong body, is catching on.

MICHELE. Brian's head on Rock's body, oh you lovely creature.

GREG. Marry me.

MICHELE. Of course, silly.

GREG stumbles forward and embraces her. At the same time, PHIL comes forward on his hands and knees to the centre. From now to the end, MICHELE is impassive, standing with the instruments.

PHIL. Went off. Right away. Weak head on weakling body. Poor me, poor leftovers. Went away, right away, live now in a cave, eat berries, talk to no one. Mornings wake up, think go for a run. Fifty press ups, bit of weight lifting. But then look down, see my weedy body, pain in the chest, acne under armpits, biceps like a baby's, balls like little marbles two a penny. So I stay in my cave all day, eat berries, talk to no one.

GREG *breaks away from* MICHELE, *and comes to the 'mouth of the cave'.*

GREG. Rock!

PHIL. In here.

GREG *'crawls into the cave.'*

GREG. Hello Rock.

PHIL. Hello, Brian.

GREG. I've left her, Rock.

PHIL. Oh yeh.

GREG. She's a monster. I lived in constant fear of further mutilations.

PHIL. You'd think she'd done enough.

A pause.

How's the body?

GREG. I can't stand it, Rock.

PHIL. Why not? That's a good body. You've not let it get run down? I'll not forgive you, if you've let it get run down.

GREG. It's very fit.

PHIL. I should hope so. I spent a lot of time on it.

GREG. It has its own momentum.

A pause.

How's the rash, under the arms?

PHIL. Know about that, do you?

GREG. Had it since I was a child.

PHIL. It's bad.

GREG. Don't scratch, that makes it worse. I thought it would be bad, I brought some Valderma.

GREG *gives* PHIL *a tube of Valderma.*

PHIL. Thanks.

GREG. Not going to put it on?

PHIL. I've not got the interest really.

GREG. No.

PHIL. No.

> *A pause.*

> What we going to do, Brian?

GREG. Could have an operation.

PHIL. Could have, I s'pose.

> *A pause.*

GREG. Could burn ourselves with petrol.

PHIL. We could.

GREG. Self-immolation.

PHIL. Yeh. I s'pose.

> *A pause.*

GREG. Seems a pity, though.

PHIL. Let's live here. In my cave. We got to face it, we're freaks. We'll live here.

GREG. What about food?

PHIL. Berries do all right for your body.

GREG. Yours cries out for meat.

PHIL. We'll knock off the occasional sheep. We may be freaks, but life can go on. Can't it? Can, can't it?

GREG. Let me see that rash.

PHIL. Let me see how the old biceps are doing.

> GREG *raises* PHIL's *arm, then squeezes some Valderma and applies it to* PHIL's *armpit.* PHIL *takes* GREG's *free arm by the wrist, and works it up and down. Both are absorbed.* MICHELE *standing with the bloody axe. The lights go down slowly.*
> *End play.*

The Education of
Skinny Spew

The Education of Skinny Spew was first presented by the University of Bradford Drama Group in June 1969 with the following cast:

SKINNY SPEW Greg Philo
MRS SPEW, etc. Michele Ryan
MR SPEW, etc. Phillip Emmanuel

Directed by Chris Parr
Stage Manager Jo Stell

It was subsequently presented by Inter-Action at the Ambiance-In-Exile Lunch Hour Theatre Club, London, on 2 March 1970 with the following cast:

SKINNY SPEW Michael Feast
MRS SPEW, etc Frances Tomelty
MR SPEW, etc Christopher Martin

Directed by Roland Rees
Stage Manager Roy Preston
Lighting by Nick Garnet

A double white sheet is laid out in the middle of a circle. When the audience are all in, the lights go down. At once a tape of a heartbeat starts. Then GREG speaks as Skinny Spew in the womb, live over a mike. Stage management make the noises of labour, written here as 'Huh', building the rhythm.

Scene One: Skinny's Birth

GREG. I think, I think I'm in some OLD BAG.

ALL. Huh.

GREG. What kind of old bag? Handbag? Paper bag?

ALL. Huh.

GREG. Whatever kind of bag, its slimy.

ALL. Huh huh.

GREG. Mother bag! A mother bag, that's what I'm in!

Stuffed in my mother's womb!

A loud BOM on a drum. At once the lights go up. MICHELE, as Mrs Spew, is lying under the sheet.

MICHELE. Ow! Doctor doctor!

PHIL comes forward as the Doctor.

Doctor doctor, he kicked and awful hard.

PHIL. Little Bobby Charlton is he? Ha ha.

MICHELE. Is he on his way?

PHIL. He's on his way. Out the dressing room, up the players' tunnel, onto the football pitch of life, ha ha.

GREG. The doctor sounds a right twit.

ALL. Huh huh.

GREG. I think, I think I'll give him a rough time. I think, I think I'll come out upside down. Or backwards.

ALL. Huh huh.

GREG. I know. I'll startle medical science and come out through her bum.

ALL. HUH HUH.

> MICHELE *writhes. She grabs the top of the sheet about her throat, in a knot, and holds on tight.* PHIL *grabs the other end, and it's a tug of war, with the sheet between* MICHELE's *legs.*

MICHELE. Doctor doctor, what's gone wrong?

PHIL. The little bugger.

MICHELE. Ow! He's wriggling about!

> *The heart beat gets louder.* PHIL *gets desperate.*

PHIL. Don't worry I'm fully qualified. Nurse! Forceps!

GREG. He thinks I'm a cork in a bottle.

ALL. HUH HUH.

PHIL. One two!

> PHIL *tugs.*

MICHELE. Ow!

GREG. Ow!

PHIL. At times like this I wonder why I ever took up surgery. Come on you little runt! One two!

> PHIL *tugs.*

MICHELE. Ow!

GREG. Ow!

PHIL. They think a doctor's life is all beauty. One hand on the pulse of nature, the other up a nurse's skirt. One two!

> PHIL *tugs.*

MICHELE. Ow!

GREG. Ow!

PHIL. Lance a boil. Chop out some old geezer's gallstones. Drag a baby into the world bloody and puking. It's all butchery. Slash slash slash. Come on you horrible bundle of joy, come on, come on.

> *The lights are fading.* PHIL *is at full stretch tugging the sheet.* MICHELE *is screaming, the heart beat is very loud.*

ALL. HUH HUH HUH, HUH HUH HUH, HUH HUH HUH HUH.

Blackout. A short silence. The drum goes BOM. *Then* GREG *is heard on a tape, bawling his head off like a baby.*

Scene Two: Childhood

Lights up. GREG *is in the centre, in a pram. He has a teddy bear.* PHIL *as Mr Spew and* MICHELE *as Mrs Spew stand by the pram. A pause. It's a family photograph, the mother adoring, the father disgruntled, the baby scowling.*

GREG. I just got born. And that's my Mummy. And that's my Daddy. And I think, I think I'll shit my nappies up.

MICHELE. There you are Henry. Our very own little one.

PHIL. I think he's shitting his nappies up.

MICHELE. He's not. He's Mummy's little boy. And Mummy's little boy would not shitty whitty his nappy wappies.

GREG *looks around.*

GREG. She talking to me?

MICHELE. Ogy ogy goo.

GREG. She IS talking to me.

MICHELE. A little one, after all these years! Woogy woogy wiggy wiggy.

GREG. I know I'm a baby. But she's carrying on like I was a moron. I think I'll give her what for.

GREG *throws the teddy bear out of the pram.*

Waa. Waa.

MICHELE *picks up the teddy bear, and gives it back to* GREG. GREG *snatches it, and glares at her.*

PHIL. He looks a bit pasty.

MICHELE. They always look like that.

PHIL. He's got scabs on his mouth.

MICHELE. That's quite normal.

PHIL. There's snot running out of his nose.

MICHELE. That's normal too.

PHIL. I don't like the way he's glaring.

MICHELE. Henry, he's your very own son and heir. Aren't you proud?

PHIL. Evil looking bleeder.

MICHELE. He's a lovely baby. Ogy ogy.

GREG. Waa waa.

GREG throws the teddy bear out of the pram.
MICHELE picks up the teddy bear and gives it back to GREG.
GREG snatches it, and glares at her. A pause. Then PHIL sniffs.

PHIL. He has shitted himself. Ever since he came back from the hospital he's been lying there shitting himself.

MICHELE. All babies do their business.

PHIL. Not every ten minutes. Twenty-four hours a day. I tell you, he's a born trouble maker.

MICHELE. I don't know how you can say that of an innocent little babe.

GREG throws the teddy bear out of the pram.

GREG. Waa waa.

PHIL. I tell you, we're going to rue the day we had that. Rue the day.

GREG. Waa waa. I'm catching on fast. My Daddy hates my guts. I bet I was a contraceptual blunder. I bet he came home pissed, and had a faux pas with my Mum. Probably slit the rubber with his thumb nail. Waa! Waa!

MICHELE picks up the teddy bear, and gives it to GREG.
GREG looks around evilly, then tears the teddy bear apart piece by piece, with great deliberation. When he's only got the head left, there's a pause.

PHIL. He's a monster.

GREG pokes the teddy bear's eye out with his fingers, throws the head away, and makes baby noises of delight.

GREG. Gug gug gug.

PHIL. You've gone and given birth to a monster. I knew he was a monster at his christening, when he sicked up in the font. Remember what the vicar said. God Help Us!

MICHELE. Don't talk like that Henry.

PHIL. He's got an evil mind! Three weeks old and already mutilating. What's he gonna be like when he's thirty? A Frankenstein! A new Hitler! Mind you he gets it from your side. I always said your Mother was half cut.

MICHELE. Don't talk like that. He's beautiful.

GREG *puts his tongue out at* PHIL.

PHIL. He'll have to go! We'll parcel him up. In newspaper. Dump him at the gates of Buckingham Palace.

MICHELE. You never wanted a little one. Did you?

PHIL. He's one big accident.

MICHELE. Your own son, unwanted by you.

PHIL. One big mistake.

MICHELE. And whose?

A pause.

PHIL. I knew you'd bring that up. I knew you'd bring that up.

MICHELE. You no good lower class lout.

PHIL. Bringing it all up aren't you.

MICHELE. I am. I will. From now on till your dying day. You had your fun.

PHIL. My conjugal right weren't it? Fun.

MICHELE. And now you pay the price. Him!

GREG *gives* PHIL *a 'V' sign.* PHIL *is suddenly tired.*

PHIL. Oh, go and change his nappies.

MICHELE. Don't you worry my lovely. He'll not dump you at any palace door.

MICHELE *wheels* GREG *off.* PHIL *is left standing there.*

Scene Three: On Bridlington's Sand.

PHIL. I fumbled, that's all. Every man does, from time to time.
Fumble.

He protests.

I was young! A randy blighter! Ethel was a fun-loving chick.
And not a care had either of us. We married blithely, in a
smoochy mood. It were all roses, and kisses, and a lover's
moon, and Frank Sinatra singing 'Strangers In The Night'.

A pause.

But a few years on, and she got varicose veins. False teeth.
Bunions the size of oranges. And she started going on about
a kid. That she were fast getting by the age of bunning up.

He begins to roll up his trousers to the knees.

But I didn't want a kid. The joys of fatherhood I saw as a
pain in the neck. Eagerly to be avoided. In my mind I was
still a randy blighter. In my mind.

*When he has rolled his trousers up, he pauses for a few of his
words, then lays the sheet carefully out in front of him,
smoothing the wrinkles.*

She gave up precautions herself, Saying if nature's course was
to be stopped, I was to do it. And I . . . Fumbled.

He sits down, facing the sheet.

He leads us a terrible life. I've given up. I just do what the
little cunt says. He said he wanted to go to the seaside. That's
why we're here. On Bridlington sands.

PHIL *takes the edge of the sheet and slowly flicks it, making
a wave effect.* MICHELE *comes on as the mother, who's
raddled and weary now. She leads* GREG *as Skinny by the
hand. He carries a bucket and spade.*

GREG. Oh look! A silly crab.

GREG *stamps on it.*

Oh look! A silly starfish.

GREG *stamps on it.*

Oh look! A silly . . .

GREG *is about to stamp on it, but withdraws.*

Jelly fish.

At once, to PHIL.

Dad, can I have your lighter? Burn up this silly jellyfish.

MICHELE. Skinny, why you want to harm those creatures?

GREG. Cos they're there.

MICHELE. They've got as much right to be there as you have.

GREG. They not!

MICHELE. WHY not Skinny?

GREG. Cos I say not!

MICHELE. Oh dear.

PHIL *wearily*.

PHIL. Having the time of his life, is he? Beats me why he wanted to come to the bleeding seaside. Screamed his head off about it for weeks. Now he's here, what does he do? Scream his head off.

GREG. Shut your cakehole fish face.

PHIL. What did you say?

GREG. I said can I have a fresh ice.

PHIL. You did not. You said . . .

PHIL *makes a gesture of despair*.

Oh, stuff it.

GREG. Stuff what Daddy?

MICHELE. Oh dear.

GREG. I wanna go wee wee!

MICHELE. Oh Skinny, we passed a gents back under the pier. Why didn't you say so then?

GREG. Cos I didn't want to. Then.

PHIL. Better take him back Ethel.

GREG. I wanna go wee wee . . .

GREG *points at the sheet*.

In the sea!

PHIL. You cannot wee wee in the sea.

GREG. Why not!

PHIL. Cos, you horrible little boy, that is a contravention of the local byelaws relating to public hygiene.

GREG. In the sea! In the sea!

MICHELE. Better let him, Henry.

PHIL. Oh all right. Let him poison the coastline. Let thousands of bathers perish. I don't care. Anything for peace and quiet.

GREG. Goody goody goody.

GREG *'wades in'*.

Look at the animal!

MICHELE. What we going to do with him, Henry?

PHIL. I don't know, Ethel.

GREG *is 'in the sea', that is he has the sheet around him, and he's sitting down with his legs out straight.*

GREG. Look at 'em, two old boots on the seashore. I know what they're thinking. They're thinking they've just about had enough.

PHIL. I've just about had enough, Ethel.

MICHELE. I know, Henry. But what we going to do?

GREG. An' I bet, I bet they're getting round to thinking of putting me away.

PHIL. I'm getting round to thinking of putting him away.

GREG. Ha! They don't know even in the womb, I heard 'em. I caught on EARLY.

PHIL. He may be simple. He may be a bloody genius. But either way he's a little sod, and I can't cope.

MICHELE. I can't cope.

PHIL. Neither of us can.

MICHELE. No.

PHIL. Cope.

A pause.

PHIL. They have . .

A pause.

Places for 'em.

GREG. They want to put me in a place with nuts! But they won't get away with it. They don't know I GOT A PLAN.

GREG goes on his back, and wriggles under the sheet, waving his arms.

Mummy, Mummy, help.

MICHELE. It's Skinny!

GREG. Mummy, help.

MICHELE. He's drowning!

PHIL. He's having you on.

GREG. I'm drowning Mummy.

MICHELE. He is! I'm coming, my one and only!

MICHELE 'swims' to GREG. GREG suddenly appears from under the sheet, and grabs her neck.

GREG. You going to put Skinny away, Mummy?

MICHELE. Skinny let go of my neck!

GREG. Put Skinny away?

MICHELE. You're so heavy Skinny. OH . . .

MICHELE disappears under the sheet. She makes muffled bubble noises.

GREG. Daddy, Mummy's drowning.

PHIL. Oh my God! Hold on Ethel, my one true love!

PHIL 'swims' to GREG. GREG suddenly grabs his neck.

GREG. Going to put Skinny away, Daddy?

PHIL. Let go my neck you great freak!

PHIL disappears under the sheet, joins MICHELE in muffled bubbles and cries of 'Skinny'. GREG 'swims ashore.' No more sound or movement from under the sheet.

GREG. I drowned my Mum and Dad, and now I'm free!

The lights begin to fade.

And I'll kill off all the other Mums and Dads. No more fathers, beating up their kids! No more mothers, screeching! All over the age of ten, I'll kill off too. And the world will be all PLAY.

And everyone will pee in the sea, whenever they want.

The lights are very nearly out.

Scene Four: At Major Buggery's Orphanage

The light is very low. GREG *is continuing his speech.*

GREG. That were my plan. Be Dictator Of The World! But it didn't work out. An' they put me in an orphanage.

At once the lights slam up, a bell clangs, PHIL *comes out from under the sheet as The Major, zipping up his flies,* MICHELE *comes out from under the sheet smoothing her skirt down.*

MICHELE. Oh! Major!

PHIL. Run along Matron.

MICHELE. Yes Major.

PHIL. Major Bertram Buggery signing on. Head Warden, Queen Elizabeth Home For Orphaned Little Bleeders. Trouble with nippers is, they've all got their minds on it. And I got to get their minds off it. And my recipe is, cold porridge for breakfast, cold toast for tea, and cold showers morning noon and night. That's what made me the man I am, Gad.

PHIL *clutches his leg.*

Oh my bally leg.

MICHELE *comes forward, dragging* GREG *by the arm.*

MICHELE. Come on Skinny Spew. You're going to see the Major.

MICHELE *mimes going to the door, and knocking.*

The new boy, Major.

MICHELE *shoves* GREG *through the 'door'. A pause. Then* GREG *rushes forward and kicks* PHIL's *bad leg and makes a getaway.*

PHIL. Trod on me gouty leg, the dirty little hun! Dial 999!

MICHELE *mimes dialing a telephone.*

GREG. Kicked the old git. Dived through the window. Hid in the grounds. Waited until dark, then made it to the by-pass.

Scene Five: By-Pass

GREG *thumbing a lift.* PHIL, *as a car and its driver, passes him, screeches to a halt, and reverses back.* PHIL *mimes opening the passenger's door.*

PHIL. And what's a little man like you doing all alone?

GREG. I wanna go to London.

PHIL. Ooo. Know your own mind, don't you.

GREG. I'm going to burn down the Houses of Parliament.

PHIL. Ooo.

GREG. And rule the World.

PHIL. You better jump in, then.

> *They drive a few yards. Then* GREG *sprawls into the centre, as if thrown from the car.* PHIL *steps aside.*

GREG. And the man in the car, went funny. And left me in a wood.

> PHIL *does a creepy owl whistle.*

GREG. And this big police lady, with a big police dog, she got me.

> PHIL *goes down on all fours as savage police dog advancing on the scene.* MICHELE *as a horrid policewoman, holding the dog back. From here the lights begin to fade to the end.*

MICHELE. Where are yer? He can smell yer, so can I yer sniveller.

> PHIL *barks.*

GREG. An' they all got me. The dogs. The coppers. And Major Buggery an' the Matron. An' the old queen on the by-pass. An' they all got me, an' got at me, cos they couldn't let me grow. What I was. The Mums and Dads, could not let me grow.

> *From here* GREG *slowly recoils, wrapping the sheet around him.* PHIL *and* MICHELE *speak with their own voices over him, quiet, deadly, kind.*

MICHELE. You bad boy. You need education.

PHIL. Bad boy.

MICHELE. We know you're bad.

PHIL. Because we're better than you.

MICHELE. So eat up your food.

PHIL. Don't slop it now.

MICHELE. Say your prayers.

PHIL. Don't mumble them now.

MICHELE. Do your sums.

PHIL. Get them right now.

MICHELE. Learn all the letters of the alphabet.

PHIL. And be good.

MICHELE. Be good.

> *From under the sheet* GREG *makes gug-gug, baby like sounds.*
> *He's regressed. A tape of a real baby really crying drowns*
> *him, and the fading light reaches blackout.*
> *End play.*

Methuen's Modern Plays

Jean Anouilh	*Antigone*
	Becket
	The Lark
John Arden	*Serjeant Musgrave's Dance*
	The Workhouse Donkey
	Armstrong's Last Goodnight
John Arden and	*The Business of Good Government*
Margaretta D'Arcy	*The Royal Pardon*
	The Hero Rises Up
	The Island of the Mighty
	Vandaleur's Folly
Wolfgang Bauer,	*Shakespeare the Sadist*
Rainer Werner	
Fassbinder,	*Bremen Coffee,*
Peter Handke,	*My Foot My Tutor,*
Frank Xaver Kroetz	*Stallerhof*
Brendan Behan	*The Quare Fellow*
	The Hostage
	Richard's Cork Leg
Edward Bond	*A-A-America!* and *Stone*
	Saved
	Narrow Road to the Deep North
	The Pope's Wedding
	Lear
	The Sea
	Bingo
	The Fool and *We Come to the River*
	Theatre Poems and Songs
	The Bundle
	The Woman
	The Worlds with *The Activists Papers*
	Restoration and *The Cat*
	Summer
Bertolt Brecht	*Mother Courage and Her Children*
	The Caucasian Chalk Circle
	The Good Person of Szechwan
	The Life of Galileo
	The Threepenny Opera
	Saint Joan of the Stockyards
	The Resistible Rise of Arturo Ui
	The Mother
	Mr Puntila and His Man Matti
	The Measures Taken and other
	Lehrstücke
	The Days of the Commune

	The Messingkauf Dialogues
	Man Equals Man and *The Elephant Calf*
	The Rise and Fall of the City of
	Mahagonny and *The Seven Deadly Sins*
	Baal
	A Respectable Wedding and other one act plays
	Drums in the Night
	In the Jungle of Cities
Howard Brenton	*The Churchill Play*
	Weapons of Happiness
	Epsom Downs
	The Romans in Britain
	Plays for the Poor Theatre
	Magnificence
	Revenge
	Hitler Dances
Howard Brenton and	
David Hare	*Brassneck*
Shelagh Delaney	*A Taste of Honey*
	The Lion in Love
David Edgar	*Destiny*
	Mary Barnes
Michael Frayn	*Clouds*
	Alphabetical Order and *Donkey's Years*
	Make and Break
	Noises Off
Max Frisch	*The Fire Raisers*
	Andorra
	Triptych
Simon Gray	*Butley*
	Otherwise Engaged and other plays
	Dog Days
	The Rear Column and other plays
	Close of Play and *Pig in a Poke*
	Stage Struck
	Quartermaine's Terms
Peter Handke	*Offending the Audience* and *Self-Accusation*
	Kasper
	The Ride Across Lake Constance
	They Are Dying Out
Barrie Keeffe	*Gimme Shelter (Gem, Gotcha, Getaway)*
	Barbarians (Killing Time, Abide With Me, In the City
	A Mad World, My Masters
Arthur Kopit	*Indians*
	Wings

John McGrath	*The Cheviot, the Stag and the Black, Black Oil*
David Mercer	*After Haggerty*
	The Bankrupt and other plays
	Cousin Vladimir and *Shooting the Chandelier*
	Duck Song
	The Monster of Karlovy Vary and *Then and Now*
	No Limits To Love
Peter Nichols	*Passion Play*
	Poppy
Joe Orton	*Loot*
	What the Butler Saw
	Funeral Games and *The Good and Faithful Servant*
	Entertaining Mr Sloane
	Up Against It
Harold Pinter	*The Birthday Party*
	The Room and *The Dumb Waiter*
	The Caretaker
	A Slight Ache and other plays
	The Collection and *The Lover*
	The Homecoming
	Tea Party and other plays
	Landscape and *Silence*
	Old Times
	No Man's Land
	Betrayal
	The Hothouse
Luigi Pirandello	*Henry IV*
	Six Characters in Search of an Author
Stephen Poliakoff	*Hitting Town* and *City Sugar*
David Rudkin	*The Sons of Light*
	The Triumph of Death
Jean-Paul Sartre	*Crime Passionnel*
Wole Soyinka	*Madmen and Specialists*
	The Jero Plays
	Death and the King's Horseman
C.P. Taylor	*And a Nightingale Sang . . .*
Nigel Williams	*Line 'Em*
	Class Enemy
Charles Wood	*Veterans*
Theatre Workshop	*Oh What a Lovely War!*

Methuen's Theatre Classics

Büchner	**DANTON'S DEATH** *(English version by James Maxwell; introduced by Martin Esslin* **WOYZECK** *(translated by John MacKendrick; introduced by Michael Patterson)*
Chekhov	**THE CHERRY ORCHARD** *(translated and introduced by Michael Frayn)* **UNCLE VANYA** *(English version by Pam Gems: introduced by Edward Braun)*
Euripides	**THE BACCHAE** *(English version by Wole Soyinka)*
Gogol	**THE GOVERNMENT INSPECTOR** *(translated by Edward O. Marsh and Jeremy Brooks; introduced by Edward Braun)*
Gorky	**ENEMIES** **THE LOWER DEPTHS** *(translated by Kitty Hunter-Blair and Jeremy Brooks; introduced by Edward Braun)*
Granville Barker	**THE MADRAS HOUSE** *(introduced by Margery Morgan)*
Hauptmann	**THE WEAVERS** *(translated and introduced by Frank Marcus)*
Ibsen	**BRAND** **A DOLL'S HOUSE** **AN ENEMY OF THE PEOPLE** **GHOSTS** **PEER GYNT** *(translated and introduced by Michael Meyer)*
Jarry	**THE UBU PLAYS** *(translated by Cyril Connolly and Simon Watson-Taylor; edited with an introduction by Simon Watson-Taylor)* **SELECTED WORKS** *(edited by Roger Shattuck and Simon Watson-Taylor)*
Molnar	**THE GUARDSMAN** *(translated and introduced by Frank Marcus)*
Schnitzler	**LA RONDE** *(translated by Frank and Jacqueline Marcus)* **ANATOL** *(translated by Frank Marcus)*

If you would like to receive, free of charge, regular information about new plays and theatre books from Methuen, please send your name and address to:

The Marketing Department (Drama)
Methuen London Ltd
North Way
Andover
Hampshire SP10 5BE